THE ORBIT OF
THOMAS MANN

THE ORBIT
OF
THOMAS
MANN

BY ERICH KAHLER

PRINCETON, NEW JERSEY

PRINCETON UNIVERSITY PRESS

1969

PREFACE

THE PAPERS collected in this book, which deal with the world of Thomas Mann and its environmental dimensions, originated in different periods; some of them were originally written in German, some of them in English. The three middle pieces, forming the core of the book, are concerned with Thomas Mann's novels and with the significance of his artistic personality. The introductory essay, *The Responsibility of Mind*, deals with the outer, social climate of Thomas Mann's development; the concluding one, *Doctor Faustus from Adam to Sartre*, with the inner, transcendental implications of the Faustus motif and Thomas Mann's role in its history.

The merit of Professor Francis Golffing's English translation of the *Secularization of the Devil, Thomas Mann's "Doctor Faustus,"* could still be appreciated by Thomas Mann himself. The superb translations of the two essays, *The Elect* and *Representation and Revolution*, by my friends Krishna and Richard Winston, remain for me to value fully. My deep gratitude is due particularly to Richard Winston for his assistance in revising *The Responsibility of Mind* and *Doctor Faustus from Adam to Sartre*.

E.K.

CONTENTS

THE ORBIT OF
THOMAS MANN

THE RESPONSIBILITY

OF MIND

THE intent of this essay is not to deal with Thomas Mann as an artist, but rather to show him in his role of a man concerned with things of the mind. Now, what exactly do we mean by a man who is concerned with the things of the mind? The English language has no word for him—it knows only the "intellectual," who is by no means identical with the "man of mind." Only the German language makes that valuable distinction between "intellectual" and "*geistig.*" An intellectual is anyone who concerns himself with the arts, the sciences, and the professions, and their practical applications; it is a concept embracing many occupations, a whole level of life, civilizational and societal. But not all artists, scholars, scientists, doctors, lawyers, engineers can be called men of mind, and to qualify as one, one need not necessarily belong to any of these societal groups. As I see it, a "man of mind" (*geistiger Mensch*) is one for whom supra-personal problems and decisions are a personal concern, one who no longer draws a line between the personal and the supra-personal, since in the depths of his being he has completely and passionately identified himself with such general concerns. For the "man of mind," understanding the world and caring about its flaws is close to the heart. In short, he is someone who feels a personal responsibility for the human condition.

3

It is this quality that I think of when I call Thomas Mann a prototype of the "man of mind." It is this human quality which we feel at the bottom of his whole work and which gives his art its specific tone and profundity. Most particularly and directly it finds its expression in his pragmatic and theoretical papers, which are closely related to his purely artistic creations, more closely related than is the case with other contemporary authors. The essays are indeed preludes, bridges, preliminary outlines, or conclusive interpretations of his narrative work. Very often, too, they are monologues whose purpose is to clarify the writer's thoughts for his own ends. In them he struggles to resolve certain unsolvable human perplexities. They are also disguised confessions.

Their sequence actually begins with that extremely problematic book which bears the significant title, *Reflections of a Non-Political Man*. The challenging title implies its opposite. For from the moment the author launched this challenge he ceased to be non-political. Since then, indeed since the First World War, it has become impossible to express anything of human concern without touching the political sphere. The world, at that time, had begun to be drawn into the great crisis which was to engulf everything and everyone.

The *Reflections of a Non-Political Man* is certainly a very questionable book; it is so not only today, it was so from the beginning. For it is a book full of questions, questions which seem to arise from the dispute with his brother but in fact are addressed to Thomas Mann himself. They reflect the perhaps somewhat belated process by which the poet and the thinker broke out of the secure realm where, especially in Germany, he could follow his contemplative calling in complete remoteness from the affairs of the day. In this book, Germany is presented as a bastion against the rest of the world, particularly the Western world. But the issues of this battle reached far beyond the personal and regional battlefield; they had a generally human import. Germany represented "culture" (*Kultur*) against "civilization": the dedication to a basic order of things and its lasting values as against the futility of material well-being. It represented everything vital, real, and genuine in opposition to esthetic, poetical, rhetorical superficiality. It stood for the realm of the mind as against pleasingly ephemeral existence, the restlessness of volatile doings and dealings. Germany stood for the timelessly essential, which had withal its hidden creative future, which would begin to dawn beyond the obsolescent world of material progress. It stood for the lonely, self-imposed responsibility of the artist, the thinker, and the statesman, rather than for public commitments and obligations. All this was comprised in the term "unpolitical" as opposed to the term "political." What was affirmed was the aristocratic, as against the democratic principle.

Yet all the foregoing was no longer a firmly held conviction. The book is in a state of continuous flux. Atavisms are at odds with premonitions, aspects are perpetually shifting, and the positions, however passionately defended, even to political extremes, seem undermined by conscious or unconscious queries. The whole book is a battle, not only with the other side, but with the writer himself, who wages a desperate struggle for calm inner certainty

5

in the midst of growing turmoil. But it was in vain; the artist was irrevocably drawn into the political sphere; whatever he touched turned political, and his fundamental problem of old—the problem of the artist's position in the world, and his relation to the world, the problem of *Tonio Kröger* and *Death in Venice*—became a burning question of the day. Thus a direction was indicated. For precisely insofar as Thomas Mann had been deeply earnest about all that the bastion Germany meant to him, insofar as this was truly his innermost concern, the contact with the political arena must have revealed to him where his place was, where he had to look for the concern for humanity, the defense of the mind and of the "future." His eyes were opened to the reality of the situation, and what followed was, step by step, an increasing belief in a social-minded, democratic republic.

Although the *Reflections of a Non-Political Man* contains many things which are no longer tenable, indeed some which were never quite tenable, it remains a memorable and praiseworthy book. For I know very few books in the literature of the world in which the spiritual drama, a supra-personal transformation reflected in a very personal struggle, with all its erring, probing, and searching, with all its passionate reflection and reflective passion, reveals itself in such moving candor. I know hardly a book from which one can learn better what it is to be a man of mind. And all the political conviction which Thomas Mann was later to express so perseveringly and fiercely would be of lesser weight had it not been won through the bitter combat of this book.

But this oscillating, ambivalent, stormy, and inconclusive book has a still broader significance. We may see in it a kind of watershed, a dividing line between two epochs. The conflicting attitudes representing these epochs disclose the precarious, indeed the tragic role of the man of mind in our time.

The growing peril threatening the artist and the thinker had been deeply felt through the whole nineteenth century from Goethe and Stendhal to Flaubert, Burckhardt, and Nietzsche. But it became a matter of immediate concern only after the First World War, when the man of mind was confronted directly and inescapably with political and social reality, when he was forced to take a stand.

Only then did the profound conflicts to which he was exposed become patently manifest. For a century the role of the masses had been growing in importance and at an ever-increasing tempo. This new development inevitably brought with it a leveling and standardization of life, a predominance of the average man, of mediocrity, of routine. There was an increasing commotion of publicity, of teeming actuality; and the lonely voice which did not shout—for the most essential and most subtle things do not lend themselves to shouting—was hopelessly drowned out. The dominance of the masses brought with it the drabness and ugliness of monotonous working-days filled with increasingly mechanized work, the atomization of human knowledge, accumulation of facts and loss of meaning. The man of mind has learned by experience that genuine creation, and indeed receptive sensibility, is gained only in slow maturation through a careful training of our senses; he knows that truth is a very delicate thing and cannot be seized by mechanical categorization, that even in its simplicity it is never simplistic, but comprehends a rich and often paradoxical complexity. He also knows that personal truth cannot thrive without a personal pattern of life. All this is incompatible with the drift toward collectivism. He is forced to recognize the damage done to the human condition by the clichés of the political battles, the careless manufacture of trash in the arts, and the proliferating specialization in the sciences; he is forced to see how the slogans of ubiquitous commercial advertising, combined with social and political propaganda, generate an atmosphere of deceit which benumbs the consciousness of the people and prevents an understanding of the real situation. The people are no longer governed by human beings with whom communication is possible, but by emotion-laden catch words, powerfully diffused by a host of mechanical means, against which the individual is helpless. It was in protest to all this that many of the best minds of the nineteenth and the twentieth centuries adopted an attitude of conservatism, with its overemphasis on individuality. This protest pushed the artist into romanticism, estheticism, epatism, hero worship, into resignation, or the ivory tower of *l'art pour l'art*; it pushed the philosopher into solipsism and Indian quietism, or nihilistic revolt. Such protests, which are sounded in the *Reflections of a Non-Political Man*, prompted quite a number of intellectuals after the First World War to become partisans of a movement that led them into an even more pernicious falsehood, a tyranny of slogans more vulgar than the one they were protesting, and ultimately lured them into outright betrayal of self.

For, on the other hand, there is no escape from the new reality for the man of mind who wants to remain true to himself. He is of necessity a revolutionary. He must aim at the new and espouse its cause—not for the sake of novelty, but because it is the future, that which is to come and which he has to perceive earlier than others; indeed he must help to bring it into being. His truth is at the frontier of the knowable; his responsibility is to what can hardly be grasped as yet, for everything is quite true only in the moment of creation. There was the new reality which had to be mastered. There was the commandment to create a democratic world; it was irrevocably pronounced with the all-pervading rationalization and socialization of life, with the rise of industry, and the concomitant claim of the growing masses. But its first result was the usurpation of control in the Western countries by the powerful forces of the capitalistic system. It is certainly not the mission of the mind to defend the world dominance of money. Hardly any other system was so detrimental to the basic human values as that of capitalism.

It was the world of the capitalistic bourgeoisie against which the protest of the mind in the nineteenth century was directed. Wearing the guise of a formal democracy that concealed the oligarchy of the financial powers, the dangerous phenomena had appeared which had aroused the disgust of artists and thinkers. Those who felt a revulsion against this state of affairs could either, like Goethe, Stendhal, the romanticists, and Carlyle, turn back to the fading era of aristocratic and heroic tradition, or, like the socialists, Tolstoy, Ruskin, William Morris, anticipate a future of social justice which would re-establish the human values together with human rights, a realm of beauty together with a realm of morality. But this was still an era when the historical process moved more slowly, and it was still possible to remain contemplative and inconsistent. It was the same Flaubert, to whom the bourgeoisie was nauseating, progress a delusion, and politics a *saleté,* who nevertheless accomplished the breakthrough into the new reality, and who with embittered fidelity and with the love-hatred of the artist described this loathed world of the bourgeoisie. The same Dostoevsky who was the bitter foe of socialism unveiled the depths of human misery which called it forth; it was he who created the concept of universal man, a concept conceivable only in a socialist order. In the nineteenth century such tacit contradictions are common to all minds of any significance; they are evident in the strikingly irreconcilable insights and prophecies of Nietzsche.

In the great crisis, however, that emerged from the First World War, the middle class began to defend itself against the growing threat of socialism with the same individualistic arguments which had been used against itself in the nineteenth century. But what had been a genuine revolutionary issue and a true belief in the struggle against oppressive feudal powers had now become a hypocritical dogma; people who had long forgotten what it means to be an individual, a fully developed human person, used the slogan of individual liberty to defend the economic system of uncurbed private enterprise, which actually had begun to be collectivized in big anonymous trusts and corporations. A manipulated democracy eked out with the mystique of nation, race, hero-worship, and "blood and soil," was mobilized to support free enterprise. In this witches' dance the man of mind was forced to take an immediate stand.

The alliance with middle-class individualism was extremely questionable and suspect. It meant joining forces opposed to the future, opposed to the new social reality, opposed to the human rights of the weak and the awakening of an ignorant and deluded people; and indeed it led to a despotism of vilest brutality and a condition of unprecedented lawlessness. On the other hand, the effects of mass existence, the drugging of consciousness through ideological slogans propagated by the new mass media, had developed further. The sense for the values of the human person, the most precious values of man, had become confounded, and threatened to vanish. The complexity of reality, its overcrowding with facts, increased in proportion to peoples' diminishing capacity for comprehending it.

All this made an old conflict in the man of mind most acute. The farther the artist and the thinker reaches in his search for the truth, the more he moves away from what can be popularly grasped. The deeper he penetrates into the hidden layers of nascent reality, the more he loses touch with the immediate present. And yet it is the present which urgently needs to be elucidated and prepared for the future. But when the results of the artist's search finally reach the broad public, after having passed through the intermediate filters of publicity, they not only have become half-truth, but have usually come on the scene too late to be effective; for the political and social developments have taken another course, a rough-and-ready one, directed by emotions, economic interests, and habitual preconceptions. What position should the man of mind then take? If he sacrifices the truth for the sake of immediate influence, he ceases to be himself, a true artist, an honest thinker. If he sacrifices influence for the sake of truth, then his efforts, which were meant to serve man, assume a slightly ridiculous and quixotic character. He must bear responsibility for what happens, for that is the essence of his being; he is even made responsible and called to account for his inability to prevent the horrors that have taken place and are taking place again and again. Still his position is nowhere officially registered and the more deeply he feels his responsibility the more private he becomes, the less he is listened to. Then, too, there is no easily recognizable mark by which he can be distinguished from his half-brothers whose influence is far greater than his.

Thus, the man of mind today seems to be faced with a twofold impossible choice: the choice between human rights and human values, which are actually inseparable, and the choice between truth and influence which are useless if separated.

In reality, he has no choice. He is confronted with the problem of concretely reconciling truth with influence, human rights with human values, or rather of conceiving an order of things in which such a reconciliation would be possible. And this is in fact identical with the problem of democracy.

We cannot go back, we can only go forward; historical processes are irreversible. We cannot preserve, we can only conquer, and, in the face of change, reconquer what is worth preserving, thereby making it new. Democracy is on its way; it is halfway here; it cannot be undone, nor curbed in its development without perpetuating and enlarging the prevailing anarchy. The leveling of standards through mass production and mass consumption, the dizzying growth of physical as well as intellectual communication, and, as a result, the ever closer interdependence of people, nations, and continents—all this leads to an increasing participation of everyone in everything. It was the capitalistic system which brought this about in concurrence and in alliance with technology, and it is irrevocably committed to expanding communication, since capitalism simply lives by expansion. Its aim must be to enable the greatest number of people to participate in consumption, and therefore—because they must be furnished with sufficient buying power—also in production and productivity. But under the capitalistic system the economic process is directed by the interest of the producers not of the consumers, in the interest of capital not of the people. Production, productivity, is the highest goal. People have to be taken into consideration inasmuch as they are actual and potential customers. They have to be kept in a state of prosperity because only then are they able to purchase, and the prosperity itself is predominantly seen in terms of salability of goods. These are the limits set to the welfare of the masses. We are well acquainted with and accustomed to the limitations. The goods must be attractive rather than good, that is to say, they have to be good only to the extent that they do not last too long and forestall the need for new wares. The goods must not be too exquisite because then they are too expensive for mass consumption, and not profitable. But they must not be too abundant either, because they then depress the market and again are not profitable. The principle of supply and demand, on which the system was originally based, is largely invalidated by the intervention of more and more aggressive advertising, which falsifies the demand. People do not know what they are going to demand, since it is no longer the determinable goods but the surprising novelty which they demand. The supply is equally artificial through corresponding manipulation.

The democracy of our day is a true child of the capitalistic system. The party machines offer the constituency their candidates, who have been chosen without regard to their qualification to govern—a broad, suprapartisan view of the world, perspicacity, prudence, integrity—but rather on the grounds of influence and means, and particularly their vote-getting capacity. The methods of political propaganda exactly parallel those of commercial advertising. The voters respond to the persuasiveness of a candidate, the intensity and wittiness of his eloquence, and to his offers and accomplishments in relation to their professional interests and needs. They have hardly any opportunity to actively participate in crucial political decisions and are therefore ill-equipped to do so. Their influence does not go beyond the act of voting and the time of election; their insight into the actual situation and the significance of current national and international problems does not transcend the horizon of their newspapers and radio commentators. These, in turn, with few exceptions, present the issues in a manner acceptable to the practical interests of their customers, the advertisers, and the economic and social group which is their audience. It is not the people, the good of human beings, on which public life pivots, but on customers. The attempt to turn this incomplete and false democracy into a full and genuine one would mean nothing other than transforming what is right for the customer into what is right for the nation and the human being.

So under present conditions the people are identical with the consumer, and though even in economic terms people's true interests are served, yet everyone judges the degree of his personal, indeed physical satisfaction by whether he gets what he wants at an acceptable price. He has been taught to yearn for ever novel things; now he desires and obtains them. Even in the social and political sphere a discrepancy arises between personal satisfaction and the common good, between the immediate and the lasting benefit. He is satisfied as a customer and deceived as a citizen. This is the crucial issue; we have reached the decisive point.

The widest gap between the demands of the customer, and the welfare of the people and of the human being, is to be found in the cultural sphere. Nowhere can one see more clearly the baneful effects of the present system. The people as customers want an education that helps them advance swiftly in their practical career; for their leisure time they want and obtain a kind of literature, film, and radio which offers entertainment, suspense, and food for their dream life. Even the serious-minded among them, who seek to inform themselves, desire, after their modern working day, material that is easy, that offers the least resistance, the superficially new which at bottom is the old. In the stupefying perpetual rush of such gratifications, which, hardly enjoyed, are already forgotten and leave behind only a jostling mass of vague impressions, how could they perceive that this flood of distractions is cheating them of their truth, indeed of their sense of truth, the highest value of their life? How should it dawn on them that with the basic values of truth all other human values are carried away, and with the values, unnoticed, also the rights of man? How could they realize that here, in this inconspicuous erosion of human nature, the horrors of modern battlefields, of bomb shelters, of torture and gas chambers have their basic origin?

Of all this they are unaware, and this applies as well to the merchants of culture who serve their customers, the teaching institutions, the publishers, the film and radio producers, the professional writers and journalists. They would not believe it possible, and even if they were conscious of it, they probably could not, under the present system, conduct themselves otherwise than they do now. For they are themselves only the extreme exponents of an attitude that characterizes the whole traditional democracy: accommodating oneself to the wishes, the artificially stimulated appetites of the customer, letting oneself be guided by the people as "public," which means the people in its most momentary, volatile, fickle condition, accepting the present state of affairs as a standard, as immutable and incorrigible, and therefore ruling out any basic changes. The technological foundations of our existence are in perpetual flux; they have gradually brought about such fundamental change that the ways by which we live are no longer true; but men are prevented from changing accordingly. Man is prevented from maintaining, indeed saving himself through transformation of his society.

The "conservatives" will say: There you have it. People are not mature enough for self-determination. They will never be mature enough; they need a guiding hand, they need the firm moral support of our good old national values, the way of life "that made our country great," the trust in God and the discipline it implies. But accepting this counsel means closing the book of history. It would mean perpetuating the hypocrisy that arose with people's incapacity to keep pace with the rapid technological and scientific changes whose benefits they enjoy without being aware of their broadly human implications.

Our only hope, however precarious, is to adopt a radically opposite policy: the people must be made more and more mature for determining their destiny. They must be enabled to understand the factors governing their lives, to foresee and shape developments instead of being pushed into them by the latest emergency. The time has passed when it sufficed to elect officials and delegates to whom one could entrust easily understandable decisions. Today, for the citizenry even to control an official's political conduct, it must have a certain familiarity with the complex issues of public affairs, with the general condition of the nation and of our world at large. How should this be effected?

We are caught in a vicious circle. To put the people into a position where they could determine the course of their life we would need a new public order, and the establishment of this new order would call for a new way of thinking, a fundamentally new orientation. But how could people reach this new orientation, how could they sustain themselves within the still existent social order in which such a new attitude means starvation? And where should this fundamental change begin to take shape? It is facile to preach, as certain uplifters do, that each one of us individually should begin with himself. Single individuals are much too weak vis-à-vis the various groups that make up our present-day society, and are firmly established in all the key positions. Nor can the individual alone wage an effective resistance against the prevailing rules of the game or withstand the magic of conformity which saturates the whole atmosphere. It is not enough to quicken the new mentality in individuals; it must be carried over from individuals to groups, for only these can, at a propitious moment, accomplish the reconstruction of our society. For all this, active support is needed. From whom can it come if not from that kind of man for whom supra-personal concerns are a personal concern, who feels a personal responsibility for the human condition? Who would be able to extend such assistance if not the man whom we have called the man of mind?

But in order to do this the man of mind will have to take upon himself a much greater burden than he has carried until now. Without relenting in his labors at the inner front, at the most advanced outposts of the expressible and thinkable, he will have to undertake the additional task of keeping in touch with the outer front of the social battles of the day. The dangerous rift between the vanguard of human consciousness and the life of the masses which developed during the last centuries and left mind without influence and society without guidance, can be reduced only if the man of mind is prepared to commit his whole existence to the task and himself form the bridge from truth to actuality. He will have, as it were, to interpret his own truth, to try and translate himself into a language that penetrates men to the human core. If he never loses sight of his mission, and if he can make it clear that his search, even at the remotest frontier, is done from human concern, and for the sake of the social whole; if he can convey to his fellow men the delicate connection between his ineluctably subtle inquiries and the problems of their daily existence, then perhaps he may move them to meet him halfway, to listen to his insights and his counsels. The man of mind will have to become militant, to ally and organize himself with his peers. For his voice to be heard, he will have to become, even as Thomas Mann has radically become, a "political man."

1945

SECULARIZATION OF

THE DEVIL:

THOMAS MANN'S "DOCTOR FAUSTUS"

THE great novels of the twentieth century, its essential books, are without exception *terminal*
books, apotheoses of the narrative form. Proust's
À la recherche du temps perdu, Gide's *Faux-Monnayeurs*,
Joyce's *Ulysses*, Kafka's great parables, Musil's *Mann
ohne Eigenschaften*, Broch's *Der Tod des Vergil*, Sartre's
Nausée, Camus' *Étranger*—each, in theme, is an inventory
of our spiritual holdings, a moral, aesthetic, and metaphysical reckoning-up of our human estate; some of them,
in form, carry abstraction to a point beyond which further
evolution seems impossible. A deep, ultimate seriousness
runs through them all, a seriousness which their ever-
present irony increases rather than diminishes. Indeed,
what is irony but the transcendence of self, a chain reaction of transcendence? Today, the spiritual, the artistic,
the human itself balances on the highest peak of danger,
"exposed on the mountains of the heart." So much has
called it into question—how could it help questioning
itself?

And indeed art has come to question its own existence
—cannot escape doing so. The last veils of fiction, the last
pretense of a divine plaything, are gone; the real thing
invades the work of art; bare reality, of more dimensions
than the individual artist can cope with, decomposes and

shatters the novel. How can the artist hope to reach the central, innermost condition of our world—which is his ultimate function—without going into its formidable factual and technical processes? How can he hope to master its growing complexity without a corresponding increase in density and abstractness of presentation, without speculative analysis and exegesis?

Thus the story loses its value as a special event and becomes a parable of the human condition; the individual character becomes a type, the symbol a model. The artist today must load the tangible with so many levels of meaning that the complete work really becomes an orchestral score requiring a conductor—and indeed have single works of art ever before enlisted so many program notes and interpretations?

"When I hear about hearing . . ." says Adrian Leverkühn in *Doctor Faustus*. "When I read about reading . . ." would be a legitimate paraphrase: the reader cannot "follow" the theme without going one level of abstraction beyond it to embrace the entire structure, for the structure has in fact become the theme—the "what" ends up as the "how."

The traditional art forms have grown problematic through external, social, and cultural evolution, as well as through internal evolution, evolution of technique; art has become its own subject matter. And since the function of the artist and the intellectual has been called into question by the moral and social events of our epoch, the artist himself is drawn into a kind of polyphonic soliloquy on his role in our world.

It is just here that we have the content of Thomas

Mann's entire work, which as a whole, bears the distinguishing traits of the great terminal books of our epoch. But in his work the terminal quality does not appear all at once; it may be watched as a process, evolving through decades.

Thomas Mann's development as a novelist comprises the whole development of modern narrative prose. He began his career with a book that, though marked by the destiny of modern art, still resembled the traditional realistic novel. Indeed, he has gone on using the comfortably circumstantial, digressive manner of the nineteenth-century novel right up into the latest, "structuralist" stages of his work—even in this last summing-up, his *Faust*. Yet what a long way from *Buddenbrooks* to *Doctor Faustus*! All that has happened to us, to the world, to art, during the last half-century, can be read in the course of this journey.

Mann's whole *oeuvre*, we have said, must be regarded as a single, consistent creation because, throughout, there may be felt in it an unconscious or semi-conscious tendency toward a structural unity of the whole. It is a dynamic macrocosm, a more and more dense and comprehensive complex of developing motifs, exhibiting as a whole a fugal character such as is otherwise found only in single novels or works of art. Just as each work gains increasing symbolic richness by the use and intensification of a leitmotif and the fusing of several leitmotifs, so on a larger scale the work as a whole exhibits the progressive exfoliation and metamorphosis of one single all-pervasive theme. Mann himself, in his autobiographical sketch, has pointed, not without surprise, to the relationships forming the magic square: *Buddenbrooks, Tonio Kröger, The Magic Mountain,* and *Death in Venice.* Yet exact correspondences of this sort are to be found throughout his entire work.

The lifelong central theme of Mann's books has been an inquiry into the function of art and the artist, of culture and the intellectual in modern society. This cluster of problems had its origin in the nineteenth century, rising out of the Industrial Revolution and the political changes attendant on it, out of the mechanization, collectivization, standardization of our world, and the increasing alienation of the artist from his society.

At first the artist took a stand for threatened culture: defensively in romanticism and aestheticism; aggressively in dandyism and insolent eccentricity. But gradually, almost insensibly, his attitude began to change: his own position, the nature of art and culture themselves, became problematic to him.

It was not that his attitude toward bourgeois society changed, but that he no longer supported culture unequivocally. Instead he began to lean more and more toward a new barbarism.

Even before Nietzsche we see signs of such a development. Leconte de Lisle wrote *Poèmes Barbares,* Théophile Gautier proclaimed: "La barbarie vaut mieux que la platitude." With Nietzsche the problem becomes broadly apparent, and later developments branch out in many directions. One way leads directly through the brash extremism of the Futurists, of Spengler, Klages, and Jünger, to the *trahison des clercs*; another leads to the savagely de-

23

fiant vagrancy of Knut Hamsun and D. H. Lawrence's glorification of the vital urges; a third leads to the ambivalent skepticism in matters cultural of tired aristocrats such as Hermann Bang and Eduard Keyserling; the last and most far-reaching way leads to the bold investigations of the contemporary novel.

Thomas Mann had an initial advantage as compared with other great novelists of his generation, an advantage without which he could not have covered the vast distance between realism and structuralism. The problem fundamental to the modern novel—the role of the intellectual within his society, a problem that, in the last analysis, is the problem of man generally, of the individual surviving precariously in a technological, collective, incommensurate world—was not a problem Mann had to realize and experience intellectually; it was given to him in his cradle as his primary experience of himself. He himself *was* the problem, by virtue of the contrasts of his origin, the conjunction of the bourgeois and the artistic. From childhood he bore within himself that tension which impels the basic theme of our era.

His earliest stories introduce this theme. They are all studies of outcasts: the misshapen or unfortunate, like little Herr Friedemann, the lawyer Jacoby (*Little Lizzie*), Tobias Mindernickel, Lobgott Piepsam (*The Way to the Churchyard*); the invalid, like Albrecht van der Qualen (*The Wardrobe*); the man set apart by religious exaltation, like the monk Hieronymus (*Gladius Dei*), the archetype of Savonarola (*Fiorenza*); and, as early as *The Dilettante* and Spinell (*Tristan*), the outcast as literary

24

man, the would-be artist in his illegitimate, tragi-comic opposition to life and to the social norm. Incidentally, in both *The Wardrobe* and *Tristan* we find the germ of the motif of *The Magic Mountain*: the peculiar removal from life, the isolation and insulation that goes with illness and the atmosphere of healing. The sanitarium in *Tristan* almost strikes us as a sketch for the one in *The Magic Mountain*. Even so early as this Thomas Mann was in possession of the outlines of a work that was to be precipitated by an entirely different, unforeseeable experience, his sojourn at Davos.

These stories, as well as *Buddenbrooks,* are all what is commonly called realistic fiction. They are realistic in a cruel, often painful way that points to the influence of the great Russian novelists; they seem to result from a deliberate discipline in sustaining with exact imagination the minutest circumstances of human suffering, perverted emotion, painful embarrassment. But—and this is a wholly modern aspect of Mann's style, distinguishing it from that of the Russian novelists—all these eccentric facts have been pushed to an extreme of precision, a point of caricature, where they turn into transcendent ironies. The experience of reality has become superintensive, ironically intensive. At the same time this irony has the property of creating symbols. A perfect example is the situation in *The Way to the Churchyard*: the contentious drunkard, Piepsam, tries to push the blond, young cyclist (life) from his bicycle. Later examples are Tonio Kröger in the *Moulinet des Dames*; the carious teeth of the Buddenbrooks and the senator's collapse head-first into the gutter; Mario and the magician; and so forth. These are all extreme, vicious, ironic contrasts, and their extreme irony is what makes them symbolic. They have their root in an archetypal conflict, the ironic constitution of the artist himself.

The style of every genuine artist is originally a style of personal experience; this is true of Thomas Mann in a very special sense. There is hardly another literary *oeuvre* that bears so clear an autobiographical stamp. Mann himself has told us, for instance, in his autobiographical sketch, that every single detail in *Death in Venice* is authentic, none of it fictitious. All that happens to any individual endowed with a truly personal style of experience seems to converge into an organic system of symbols and to assume an apparently inevitable relationship to his nature. This phenomenon is particularly marked in Thomas Mann, whose fundamental problem was shaped by the circumstances of his birth. Since he experiences everything under the sign of the primary tension of his being, the raw material of life almost immediately assumes for him a symbolic character. The reciprocal irony of his psychological situation, and that further irony which transcends it, sharpen the symbolism still more. This peculiar disposition, this instinctive tendency to organize all experience symbolically, seems to account for the unique organic inter-relatedness, the fugal character of Mann's entire work.

Even the works of his early, realistic period evidence a very personal system of symbolic coordinates, an irony that creates distance and transcendence. Both in *Budden-brooks* and in *Tonio Kröger*, the fundamental, personal problem is developed almost autobiographically, in the first, genealogically, from the bourgeois standpoint, in the second, individually, from the standpoint of the artist. Bourgeois and artist, each turns his gaze and inclination toward his counterpart: there is an exact correspondence between the senator Thomas Buddenbrook, who finds solace in Schopenhauer, and Tonio Kröger, with his nostalgia for the normal, blond, and respectable.

Already culture and intellect are represented as decadence, love is associated with decline; the artist is seen as a pariah from the start, iridescent with suspect hues, shading into the daemon, the invalid, the social outcast, the adventurer, the criminal; already he is stranded in the ironic situation of expressing a life he himself is unable to live. And already the multiple variations the basic theme is to undergo in the later books become discernible. Tonio Kröger's identification, somehow felt by him to be legitimate, with the swindler, foreshadows Felix Krull, swindler-by-extravagance-of-fantasy, and the blasphemous hoax of the paraphrase of *Dichtung und Wahrheit* in Krull's diary. A single metaphor of Tonio's ("mufti's no use . . .") furnishes the germ of *Royal Highness*, the outcast "upward," the sublime clown who keeps directing a performance that is being enacted without him.

From here on the motifs split and ramify and re-join, form new variations, change keys. In *Death in Venice* the conflict that had earlier appeared as an external friction between art and life is internalized; it is within the artist, indeed, within art itself: a conflict between daemon and discipline. Discipline is what preserves the artist, what justifies art and keeps it in the framework of social responsibility. Once discipline slackens, the daemon, the *eros*, breaks loose, and in the maelstrom of debauchery both art and artist are swept into sickness and death. The active counterpart of the passive Aschenbach is the magician Cipolla (*Mario and the Magician*), another outcast, deformed, but one who compensates and overcompensates his deformity—a deeper image of the artist seen as the irresponsible puppeteer of souls who uses his magic to cast people into the most unholy ecstasies. At this point the artist passes over into the demagogue, the dictator. He too is swept into perdition by his daemon, but not because of mere passivity but because of *hubris*: unlike Aschenbach, Cipolla does not let himself go or drift, but on the contrary exercises all his powers. He is a virtuoso of the will, a fiend for the sheer joy of conquest. He does not yield to his daemon but allies himself with it, indeed identifies himself with it, challenges it, incites it.

The Magic Mountain projects Aschenbach's psychic split into the world at large. The powers of the psyche widen out into whole landscapes. Magic expands into the magic mountain, into the sphere of an intellectual, morbid, irresponsible dissociation from life, where culture and nursing merge, and where the dissolution of dying over-intensifies the stimuli of life. Discipline becomes the valley of duties, of normal, responsible action. But these too —the duties, the responsibilities, the active, normal life— lead into war and final collapse.

Here, we come upon an alteration in the fundamental motif. The normality of the normal is no longer secure.

Before this, Mann's work had been dedicated to the problem of life's boundaries: by means of his various outcasts he had delimited an area of healthy, normal, insouciant life. Now he discovers signs of decay on both sides of the boundary—in the world of action as well as up there on the magic mountain. Dying is part of living as living is part of dying.

The ambivalence, the paradox of all living things, is at last revealed. *The Magic Mountain* opens out into an unanswered question: What *is* life anyway? What is normal? What is man and where does he stand? What is the norm of man and his measure? Goethe's question is raised once more (in a world terribly changed)—the question of *Tasso*, of *Iphigenie*, of the *Elective Affinities,* of *Faust.*

Through all of Thomas Mann's books after *The Magic Mountain*, there runs the persistent motif of conflict between the abnormal and the supposedly normal, an anxious question as to the being and becoming of man. The *Joseph* novels open up the remotest layers of our mythical, totemistic past, which are at the same time the darkest layers of our psyche, the underworld of savage urges, lying ever in wait within us. Joseph rises out of these regions in a long, precarious process of sublimation, and there rises with him, within him, the sublimated, spiritualized God-image—he being the prefiguration of Jesus. He too bears a stigma from the beginning, the stigma of Grace. Grace again is full of abysses and wiles, and great discipline is required of its possessor. But, for one supreme moment, the norm seems to have shifted to spiritual man.

For one moment only. Joseph's counterpart was to appear, the Antichrist, the man stigmatized by the *curse* of spirit: Faustus.

The presentation of the Apollonian genius in *Lotte in Weimar* (*The Beloved Returns*) forms the transition. The image of Goethe emerges intact, "great, serene, and wise," as "a sacrifice—and bringer of sacrifice"; genius is preserved as an object of our reverence, sublimated as "simply the face of man." All this is still in the vein of Joseph. But behind it we see the cost, the full measure of Goethe's, of the artist's, sacrifice: not only the mastering of a world increasingly packed with factual material, of days crowded with labor, and of a refractory audience, but also the ruining of many people, among them those closest to him, and the abandoning of his own everyday humanity. Discipline once more, but now implying distance, alienation, and the chill of an uncanny, transcendent irony. This brings us to Faustus, who is entirely governed by this coldness.

I have called *Faustus* the final chapter of a terminal *oeuvre*.

To start with, it gathers together all the variations and filiations of the fundamental motif, relates them in a new way, tests one against the other, and reduces them all in magnificent concentration to the old dominant theme. For what else is this Faustus but a cosmic Tonio Kröger, a Tonio Kröger expanded to his ultimate epochal and human significance? Faustus represents the extreme, the most mature fruit of the arch-problem, the arch-experience. The psychological split is portrayed through two characters: Adrian Leverkühn and Serenus Zeitblom— the intellectual adventurer and the "healthy" bourgeois.

The character who lives a normal life writes the biography of the one who, in the simple, human sense, is not allowed to have a life. In Adrian, Tonio Kröger's primary alienation from life, his ironic detachment from it, is pushed to its metaphysical limits. Aschenbach's daemon, which operates through love and sickness, and Cipolla's daemon, which operates more subjectively as *hubris* and defiant self-aggrandizement, are united in Adrian's devil. Daemon and discipline are no longer seen as opposites, but discipline comes to serve the daemon. Between daemon and discipline, impulse and reason, death and life, there goes on the same mystical dialectic, the same reciprocal intensification that we found in *The Magic Mountain*. Besides, Adrian is really Joseph's counterpart, his spiritual kin. Adrian's elevation leads to perdition, whereas the "Pit" leads Joseph to glory; the sublimation which in Joseph's case is an act of God, in Adrian's case is an act of the Devil. From a different point of view Adrian, the Dionysian musical genius, is a counterpart of Goethe, the Apollonian, visual genius. Here too the opposites betray affinity, for both are in each: in Goethe the dark, romantic, Faustian impulse; in Adrian the lucid, visual, rational grasp of the whole. But in the last analysis the blessing and the curse seem to be contained in the contrast between word and sound, poetry and music.

Faustus is also a terminal book in point of style, the ultimate precipitation of Thomas Mann's artistic discipline. I have already intimated how this discipline, which is of North German, Hanseatic, Prussian provenance, developed through artistic filiations and the irony of an inner tension into a symbol-creating property. Discipline in art must necessarily express itself in a sharpened sense of form, an intensive striving for organic wholeness, and that means to see things symbolically.

From without, from Richard Wagner and Tolstoy, came the suggestion of the leitmotif, which in *Tonio Kröger* is already transferred from characters to ideas. Mann tells us that in *Tonio Kröger* he for the first time conceived of narrative composition as a texture of ideas woven of various themes, as a musical nexus—his affinity to music was very strong from the outset. Out of such a musical conception grows the fugal character of the later works and of his *oeuvre* as a whole.

But *Faustus* can hardly be compared any longer to a fugue; it is almost—if we may apply musical terms to a literary composition—what Adrian calls a "strict movement." It is a structure in which each detail has an exact symbolic reference, a structure of utter complexity, in which not only the various dimensions and layers, but within these each sub-motif and minor variation, is related to the rest and back to the fundamental motif. In spite of the semblance of ease in both invention and narrative, nothing here is accidental, nothing stands for itself alone; everything refers to everything else, each detail is determined by the whole. Correspondences run backwards and forwards, between beginning and end, upper and lower levels, in a kind of labyrinthine mathematics. From Buchel to Pfeiffering; from the father's "speculating on the elements" to the son's *Symphonia Cosmologica* and his fantastic excursions into the galactic and submarine spheres; from his actual mother Elsbeth to Mother Manardi and the ultimate mother Schweigestill; from Stallhanne to the maid Walpurgis; and from the laughing dog Suso, through the black swine at the entrance of the devil-house in Palestrina, to the dog Kaschperl (one of the devil's nicknames); from the dog's laugh to Adrian's bent for laughter and the tendency of his music to parody and "sardonic deviltry"; from the clear-wing moth to the whore; from the "greedy drop" and the osmotic, heliotropic pseudo-creatures to the pathological lumbar migrations of the spirochetes and to the mannikins of the *Gesta Romanorum*; from Dürer's "Apocalypse" to Kleist's *Puppet Show*; from the destiny of Adrian's doctors to that of the Rogge sisters; and from the divines of Halle to the intellectuals of Munich who smirk at the bankruptcy of the intellect—among all these a net of converging relationships is woven, and one rational and daemonic system contains them all. Even the most casual incident has its place: an emerald ring is engraved with a plumed serpent whose tongue is feathered like an arrow; an outing into the Bavarian mountains leads to Linderhof, the castle of a mad, possessed king.

The great drama of Tonio Kröger as Faustus, the drama of modern art and Germany, mirrored by the humble scribe Serenus—the impotent subject and onlooker—truly images the deeply involved Thomas Mann, ever present in the background. It is enacted simultaneously on all levels, no less in the theoretical discussions and spiritual ventures of musical technique than in syphilis, murder, and madness. The same disquieting suspense

informs the descriptions of musical scores and the biographical sections; indeed the climactic boldness of the
musical compositions comes to stand for the biographical
climax.

We need not be surprised if readers shake their heads
over the minute descriptions of a kind of music that has
never been written and perhaps never could be written.
People will ask: Is this necessary? Is this possible? It was
necessary, and it has been done. It is both legitimate and
necessary. A reader who wishes to be spared the reading
of the theoretical discussions and technical details may
as well spare himself the reading of the book altogether;
there is no other way of penetrating to its innermost
meaning. The time is past when writers could give credibility to artist-characters by letting them work for years
at some monumental literary idea in color or sound and
then having them perorate about the work, as Haupt-
mann and even Ibsen did with their artist-characters.
While this procedure has always been false and thread-
bare, today it has become quite impossible. The progression of man today, the progression of mind, is through
technical processes, and it is through them that we must
seek it and understand it.

Thus the channelling of events through technical
processes is not a sign of weakness or arbitrariness, not
mere caprice, but an imperative requirement of the total
structure giving the literary work its power of persuasion.
For at the center of this book lies the problem of the
destiny of artistic genius and of art itself.

But what happens in and to Adrian comprises not only

the fate of modern art and the intellectual; it comprises also the tragedy of Germany that is enacted in the background, the transgression of the German character, of which Adrian partakes; it comprises the general crisis of our world. The narrative takes place within three overlapping time-spans: the time-span of Adrian, 1885 to 1941, which is extended backwards into the historical depths of medieval Germany and the German Reformation by means of the spiritual climate of Kaisersaschern, where Adrian spent his childhood and by means of the humanistic-pietistic university town of Halle, where he studied; the time-span of the Third Reich, whose period of incubation coincides with Adrian's prime, and whose triumph and fall Zeitblom witnesses with horror even as he writes the story of Adrian's life; finally, our own epoch, which has given birth to the crisis of modern art and of the intellectual, and which is continuing even as we read.

All these time-strata are not only homologous but also variously interconnected. Thus the chronicle of German political events, inserted at intervals by Zeitblom into his biography of Adrian, is sometimes cross-connected with that biography, as in the discussions of the students at Halle and of the Munich intellectuals, or in the appearance of the impresario Fitelberg, who confronts Germanism with Judaism.

At the same time the book is interwoven with strands of Thomas Mann's personal history; there are long passages that are more nakedly autobiographical than any other writing by this author, who throughout his career has drawn so largely on his own life. Kaisersaschern,

35

its form and atmosphere, the "witches" in its streets, point toward Mann's native city, Lübeck; Palestrina is the place where, under virtually identical circumstances, Thomas Mann wrote his *Buddenbrooks*. Pfeiffering and Munich both evoke familiar scenes. Mann's family, his friends and acquaintances have been introduced into the story barely disguised, in some cases without change of name, in the fashion of montage.

This bold and rather disturbing procedure—apart from the lure and significance of parody—has the character of a radical confession of self. It is as though Thomas Mann wished to emphasize that he belongs in the story, is a part of it, that the destinies of Leverkühn and Zeitblom as well as of Germany, the intellectual, and modern art, deeply involve him. This *pro domo* applies not only to the author but also to the work. The compulsive tendency toward irony and parody in Adrian's creation; his rejection of make-believe and the "divine game" which leads to the self-abolition of art; the "never-relaxed, perilous playing of art on the edge of impossibility"; its "pilgrimage on peas"; its "strict counterpoint"; "the highest and strictest organization, a planetary, cosmic norm"; the "universal unity of dimensions"; the "calculation raised to mystery"; and finally the "thrust from intellectual coldness into the adventure of new feeling," the desire for "an art without suffering, psychologically sound, far from solemn, serenely intimate," "an art on terms of closest familiarity with mankind," and the conviction that the spirit "even in its most daring sallies, researches, and ventures, which seem to remove it from the common taste, can nevertheless count on serving humanity, and, in the end, in a very roundabout way, even actual people . . ."—all this is the self-projection not only of the author, it is the self-projection and self-reflection of the book. If we listen closely we may even catch in the cruel narrative that *vibrato* of the voice attributed to Adrian when he speaks with a half-modest, half-haughty casualness of the artist's ultimate familiarity with mankind.

It is Serenus Zeitblom who serves to strengthen confessional to the point of self-interpretation. True, he is the author's other half, the Overbeck of the Nietzschean Adrian, a second-remove ironic reflection of the normal on the abnormal, but his true function goes far beyond all this. He is the mediator between the various spheres, not only between Adrian and life, but also between the book and the world. He is a loose personification of the author's symbolic conscience, the commentator whose fears and forebodings, queries and meditations furnish the necessary cross-references—perhaps too many and too explicit for the acute reader, yet still hardly enough for those obtuse to symbolism. It is he who provides the additional experience of the German tragedy and integrates it with the rest; who, with his numerous reservations and confidences, makes the highly wrought craftsmanship seem easy and unobtrusive, and effects the transition to human emotion.

The creation of this character enabled Thomas Mann to maintain his highly synthetic Adrian, this cosmic figure, within the context of humanity, to make of him a real and moving character, though this is accomplished a little at the expense of Zeitblom, who often feels and expresses things that are actually outside his pale. However, the author has tried in advance to give psychological credibility to these deviations—and, indeed, man is an unstable, vibrant substance whose hidden depths may be stirred to unforeseeable effects by certain crises and stimuli. Furthermore, in this book psychology no longer counts. Zeitblom is a voice, ultimately the author's voice: "I am too close to my subject . . . but when things become serious art is left behind. . . ." Of course this itself is artifice, but it passes over into truth.

This monumental undertaking is terminal also in that it truly represents the contemporary version of the Faust problem. Valéry's *Faust*, which plays with very similar ideas, is but a fascinating existentialist idyll compared with this. Thomas Mann brings this representative symbol, not only of German but of Western culture, up to date. He treats it with finality, secularizing it and its daemon, and integrating it in a purely mundane cosmos. Redemption here has become synonymous with integration. This means that the Faustian drama is revealed as the dialectical predicament of every creature, the inborn paradox of life.

This process permeates all levels of the book. Adrian's Faustian character is constitutional. The daemon resides *within him* from the start, in his migraine, in his enormous intelligence which rapidly assimilates all that can be known. Thence ennui, the challenge to the ever more sublime, ironic transcendence, risibility, and a coldness both somber and blasé. The daemon also surrounds him, in the father who "speculates on the elements," in the medieval German climate of Kaisersaschern, in the latent polyphony of the vast collection of musical instruments in his uncle's warehouse and the growing lure of the mathematical magic of music. The genius of the stammering organist Kretschmar and the example of Beethoven carry him further, further still the theological studies at Halle, which Adrian chooses partly out of ascetic conceit, partly as a supreme feat of self-mastery, a braving of the highest powers.

For theology is a highly charged, daemoniac field of force. It survives in our modern world as a last island of medieval spirituality, a twilight area of magical dialectics and dialectical magic. This accounts for its deep affinity with mathematico-magical music. The daemon takes on greater reality in two professors of divinity, Kumpf and Schleppfuss. The baroque and blustering Kumpf, after the manner of Luther, throws bread rolls at the devil lurking in the corner of his room. But Schleppfuss, who proves by slippery, keen logic the interdependence of good and evil and the verity of witchcraft, represents, as his appearance and name indicate, the Evil One himself.

In Leipzig, whither Adrian goes later to pursue his musical studies—the attraction of music proving more concrete and immediate—the daemon finally assumes an active and decisive role and starts intervening, from within as well as from without. Adrian's proud superiority, his sensitive intellectuality and primal alienation are associated with an extreme chastity, a chastity more innocent because more naive than the pious and shrewd chastity of Joseph. It contains both a touching childlikeness and an element of cold pride.

It is just this kind of rarefied innocence that invites the deepest humiliation by sex and a consequent involvement in guilt. Indeed this presumptuous intellectuality, this ironic transcendence, constitutes in itself the Fall. The porter in Leipzig who guides Adrian to a brothel instead of a restaurant is merely an instrument of the inner daemon. Love flares up at the most casual physical contact, the purest love—with a whore, love returned even from the swamp, and this love, love from the first closed to the genius, contains the poison, the demoniac involvement, the Mephistophelian pact—that in reality was concluded from birth.

Original Sin has its way; the love-poison is consumed, consciously, despite all warnings. The pact is sealed, partly out of a genuine commitment to love, partly out of proud defiance, the innate urge to self-enhancement, to the supreme act of challenge. This monstrous union of the highest with the lowest, the most solitary with the most promiscuous, of genius with *vulgus*, this union—fulfilment and treason in one—constitutes one of the most moving love stories in world literature. It also contains in germ the manifold meaning of this powerful book.

From here on tragedy takes its predestined course. The wanton, ghastly dialogue with the Devil in Palestrina, while ostensibly the center of the book, only expresses what has been clear from the beginning: "Thou shalt not love."

And another thing it makes utterly clear is the primary determinance, the biological conditioning of the spiritual drama. "You see me," says the Devil, "therefore I exist for you. Is it worthwhile asking whether I really exist?

Is not that which acts actual? Is truth not that which is felt and experienced?" Thus hallucination and reality have equal validity, and the fellow lolling on the sofa speaks both from within and from without. The coldness that emanates from him is nothing else than the reflection of the spiritual coldness of Adrian, of that white heat that feels like ice to the touch; and the Mephistophelian wit is nothing else than Adrian's own irony. It is the same with all subsequent events: the ruin of the amorous friend whom Adrian, at once bashful and diabolic, sends as his suitor to the girl they both love; the girl's recoil; and, in his house, the death of his little nephew, the dearest of all to him, the last, tenderest Eros; set over against these, the spiritual closeness of the woman who instinctively keeps herself at a distance, whom he never sees—concord only between strangers: it is all emanated by force of that inner magic in a person which has the property of creating destiny all around itself.

Adrian's Faustian drama is set entirely within the being of spiritual man. The old cosmic drama between Heaven and Hell has been transferred into the human heart. Even the voyages into the stellar system and the submarine world are phantasmagoria nourished by science. The theological conflict is secularized; God and the Devil are secularized and made to dwell in a single body.

How naively chaste, how allegorically pure was Goethe's tragedy by comparison! There the theological element pervaded the whole cosmic scene, good and evil were neatly separated, and man was endowed with free choice. This contemporary *Faustus* is likewise full of theology, but theology has become a small, atavistic residue, a medieval remnant, revealed as a deeply suspect region where God and Devil fluidly merge, are mutually dependent, where the good is a *fleur du mal* and vice versa.

The Faustian man has stepped over into the secular realm of art, and his fate becomes the very fate of modern art, the fate of the alien intellectual in our mechanized world. His fate is inherent in his intellectuality and insofar as he is what he is, and does not deny himself, he has no longer any choice. In his very attempt to realize what is creatively true he finds himself today, together with art, together with all that is essentially human, in a diabolical plight, in the state of alienation, of the Fall—the Fall by rising, by ironic transcendence. What is good, what is bad? Sound or sick? What is innocence, if the purest—the spirit—is sin? Where lies the norm? All this has become difficult to resolve. Concepts and values are no longer immune, but have become tainted by each other.

Thus the drama is reduced to a point; event becomes stasis, becomes existence. Life's ambiguity, life's paradox, is revealed. The Devil resides in God and God in the Devil. Sublimest chastity becomes the easiest prey of the whore.

The German character, "threatened with being wrapt up in itself like a cocoon," with "the poison of solitude," beset with longings, with the urge to break into the world, is beguiled into a grab for world power that brings it nothing but the world's hatred, and suffering. The nation whose power of abstraction is the highest, whose spirituality is the most perfectly and perilously detached, the nation of Kant, Schiller, Hölderlin, plunges ahead of the rest into a sub-animal condition. This is the nation that has created the model of a modern secularized hell, where the incredible actually happens, "without any accounting," in sound-proof cellars, where torment and lust are commingled.

And what of modern art? What of this terminal book, this extreme document? Do we not find the same symptoms here? Magic has developed into the strictest structural norm, and the strictest norm—in science, too—leads back into magic. Ultimate irony, the chain reaction of transcendence, mixes with the elements and becomes deadly serious. From the furthest, cosmic, objectivity we are thrust into utter subjectivity, the confessional.

In paradoxes such as these, indeed throughout the crisis of our age, we sense the motif of Kleist's *Puppet Show*: "Thus once again we must eat of the Tree of Knowledge in order to fall back into the state of innocence." The entire effort, the supreme effort, of the contemporary spirit is directed toward this: to eat once again of the Tree of Knowledge, to make possible the impossible, redemption through union, through closest familiarity of climactic spirit with mankind. And the last hope of spirit, "the hope beyond hopelessness," "transcendence of despair," is the paradox of Grace, that salvation comes only of utter desperation.

1948

Translated from the German by Francis C. Golffing.

THE ELECT

THOMAS MANN followed up *Doctor Faustus*, the densest synthesis and most intimate statement of his central concerns, with two works of a lighter character—to all appearances satyr plays coming after the great tragedy. The first was the parable of Gregorius, the Holy Sinner; the second the confessions of Felix Krull, confidence man and fate's darling. After the supreme concentration of all his forces Mann craved relaxation; and in fact the relaxation in these two books goes very far. They are the most rollicking and high-spirited of his works.

Certainly Thomas Mann in these two works let himself go, gave free rein to his playfulness, indulged in all the intellectual games, linguistic tricks, erotic speculations, the private jokes both on himself and others which he always had in abundant store and which constituted a great temptation to him. Yet even when he lets himself go, an artist of such innate and highly developed powers of symbol-making, so disciplined a virtuoso, cannot help turning everything into form. With him, the most entertaining levity ends up as profundity.

The result is that these two books conceal extremely serious questions under that ebullient storytelling which partly delights and partly shocks the reader. The Gregorius story is in fact far more than a parody of the typical saint's legend, and *Krull* is far more than a modern picaresque novel. These tales are rich in reverberations. This essay is an attempt to register some of them and consider their meanings and interrelationships.

44

Both works, *The Holy Sinner* as well as *Felix Krull* in its expanded form, are offshoots of the central concerns of *Doctor Faustus*. For both of them again center on the problems of sin and grace, of what constitutes election.[1] Gregorius and Krull, like Joseph and Adrian, are presented to us as a pair of opposites: Gregorius is led to grace through sinfulness; Felix Krull is seduced into refined roguery by inner talents and outer good fortune. The core of these two books—as indeed of Mann's entire work—is the sense that all life on earth is deeply paradoxical, that good and evil infect one another. Mann's feeling, the consequence of contemporary upheavals, is that this mongrel creature, man, is not so simple a matter, that the moral issues are not so clear-cut as earlier ages liked to think. As Sartre has put it in *Le Diable et le Bon Dieu*, his communistic *Faust*: "Sur cette terre et dans ces temps le Bien et le Mauvais sont inséparables."

This fundamental paradoxicality glints through the surface of both stories in a thousand different guises. It is implicit in the use of a mediating narrator, almost a standard practice with Mann since *The Beloved Returns*. The face of the narrator is reflected in his own descriptions; his ambivalent emotions and comments provide an ironic frame for the story. In *The Holy Sinner* "the spirit of storytelling"—an earthly mirror of almighty Providence—is personified in a life-craving little monk who relishes all the highly indecent happenings which in the end are fully legitimized. He is a humorous counterpart to Serenus Zeitblom: "Very oft is the telling only a sub-

---

[1] The German title of *The Holy Sinner*, *Der Erwählte*, means "The Elect or Chosen One."

stitute for enjoyment which we, or the heavens, deny ourselves." In *Krull* the mediator is the protagonist himself who looks back on himself and his adventures from the vantage point of age, and enjoys them more consciously in retrospect.

In *The Holy Sinner*[2] the mighty ringing of the bells sounds the (Russian, Dostoevskian) theme on the very first page: "*Beati quorum tecta sunt peccata.*" "Blessed are they who are covered with [protected by] sins." He who would be raised to the highest sanctity must pass through deepest sinfulness. How else is the saint to acquire his knowledge of human nature? How else is the power of penance to propel man into heaven to be tested? How else, finally, is the overwhelming mightiness of Grace to be tested, if not against an overwhelming magnitude of sin? If Grace had only original virtue to contend with, it would have nothing to do. Accordingly, we are told that the kindly abbot who had taken the foundling into his care acted thus "because he knew that he was born in great sin, for that touches a Christian very near and moves his heart to a sort of reverence. . . . God has made our sin His own agony, sin and cross, they were one in Him, and above all He was the God of sinners." Grace springs from the abyss of sin, from the "hope beyond hopelessness," the "transcendence of despair."

[2] On the subjective and objective origins of *The Holy Sinner*, the connection with *Doctor Faustus* and the sources, see Mann's "Bemerkungen zu dem Roman Der Erwählte," 1951 (*Altes und Neues*, 1953) and Hermann Weigand's thorough study, "Thomas Mann's Gregorius" (*Germanic Review*, xxvii, Nos. 1-2, February and April 1952). Weigand publishes an enlightening letter from Thomas Mann to Erich Auerbach on the sources. Here we are interested only in the use to which Thomas Mann put his source-material.

But whence springs sin? In Christian dogma all sin derives from the cardinal sin of pride, man's original presumption, and in the case of Gregorius from that fundamentally anti-Christian pride of race and nobility, the arrogance of a perfectly pure lineage. The mischief begins with the simple animal pleasure of complete compatibility, with erotically charged delight in blood relationship, which offers total familiarity and the precious sense of finding oneself in the other person—for "the other" is no real other, but only a narcissistically idolized "other self." Incest is seen as a paroxysm of propinquity, of consuming propinquity which almost abolishes the polarity of love.

The Almighty wishes to demonstrate a point. There is "long hesitation" about doing this, for only after twenty years of marriage is the Flemish duchess Baduhenna doubly blessed with children. And a curse is present from the beginning, for the birth of the twins cost the mother's life. Thus the children, a boy and a girl, not only share the same birth, the same biological mystery, but they are also "death's dearest scions." Both are marked by chickenpox with identical sickle-shaped stigmata on the forehead, the brand of death stamped upon their exquisitely noble beauty. All the factors of their lives prepare them for a well-nigh inseparable intimacy, a unity in duality impervious to all outside influences. "For of us two no one is worthy," the boy Wiligis tells his sister Sibylla, "neither of you nor of me, worthy is only one of the other, since we are wholly exceptional children, high of birth . . . and born together out of death. . . ." The incest is, moreover, stimulated by the somewhat erotic partiality the widowed duke feels for his daughter. For in his "sinful nicety" he begrudges her even the most highly born suitor and sometimes takes such delight in her that he comes between her and her brother, thus arousing the boy's jealousy. Kept in bounds by the father, the adolescents' passion bursts forth on the very night of the duke's death, springing directly from his death, as it were. And as if that were not enough, the siblings' union takes place over the dead body of the faithful dog, whose howls uttered direst warning until Wiligis, in the wildness of his aroused instincts, cuts the dog's throat. A terrifying brutal deed—the chronicler calls it with full justification "the worst that happened this night . . . a spewing of love, murder and passion of the flesh, that may God pity."

From this bloody amour springs an unnamed child, burdened with the hereditary taint of incest. It must be committed to the hands of God, set sail on the sea inside a stout cask, well supplied with gold, costly fabrics, and an ivory tablet on which is written a cautious description of his noble origins, while the brother-father goes off to die on a Crusade and the sister-mother stays at home and devotes her life to penance, "a princess-nun whose heart is dead." But Providence, constantly at war with itself, pursues its cruelly paradoxical plan for the child's salvation. Providence rescues and preserves the child for further calamities. In utter ignorance, indeed through the very atoning for its existential guilt, it is driven still deeper into sinfulness, into the greater guilt of Oedipus.

Fishermen from the Island of St. Dunstan save the infant from the waves. The friendly abbot Gregorius stands godfather to the child and takes him under his wing. The boy Grigorss is reared in a fisherman's hut and then in the monastery. His physique and disposition reveal his noble origins. Despite his more delicate constitution he comes off better than the robust fishermen's boys in competitive games because of his intense discipline. "He understood better than they did how to pull himself together." Yet nobility has a flaw, the flaw of alienation, which dogged all of Thomas Mann's heroes since Tonio Kröger. The fishermen's children see this mysteriously superior and scholarly boy, this "thief of strength," as an outcast who does not belong among them. The feeling culminates in a decisive challenge from his milk-brother Flann, who feels a surge of rage at finding Grigorss reading a Latin book on the beach. Every phase of the ensuing fist fight is described in language charged with significance. Making a defensive movement, Grigorss involuntarily lands a blow on his opponent's nose. Flann is disadvantaged by his own brute strength and hatred, and Grigorss breaks his nose with a signet ring he is wearing. The ring is incised with an emblem of the lamb with the cross—the gentle one vanquishes the strong. This crisis leads to a further crisis in Grigorss' knowledge of himself. The fisherman's wife, distraught by her son's injury, cries out that Grigorss is a foundling and not her real child. What he had long unconsciously sensed, uncomprehendingly and with strange sorrow, is now confirmed. Like Tonio Kröger he had longed to overcome the qualities in himself that separated him from the harmless, normal people; now he knows that he does not belong among them. The abbot feels compelled to complete the revelation and let him read the description of his sinful origins. Grigorss is thereby launched upon his "quest for himself" and his origins, on his crusade to atone for his parents' guilt "by turning through all my life to other blood and as knight striving for its need." If nobility carries a flaw, the flaw of alienation, the Christian inversion now comes into force: "Where there is flaw, there is nobility."

Again, with hypocritical resistance to its own intentions, Providence opposes itself when the abbot begs Grigorss to remain and atone for inherited guilt as his pious and beloved successor within the cloister's peaceful walls. But Providence must know what it really intends to do with the young man, and cannot be unaware that it has introduced into his blood that knightly character which for the time being wins out over religious vocation.

Providence has also arranged the other side of the matter: Duchess Sibylla's bitter self-chastisement has kept her from taking a second husband. One aspect of this radical penance is only another expression of her old arrogant repudiation of "the other"; forbidden to love her brother, she will have none of love and marriage altogether. She thereby embroils her country in the "wooing war," when the affronted Roger of Arelat, determined to force the duchess to accept his suit, falls upon Sibylla's land and overruns it with fire and sword. Thus on both sides the constellation is prepared for the second abominable sin.

Young Grigorss is outfitted as a knight and adopts the fish for his crest—the symbol of both St. Peter and the sea. In his fine ship he sets out across the Channel, over the same waters that he drifted in as a baby, rocked by the seemingly errant waves. Now he drifts once more toward the mainland through a dense fog, projection of his own uncertainty. Once ashore, he immediately finds what he has wished for: innocence in distress in the form of a lady "wonder-strange" and "wonder-near" who must be delivered from dire peril. He delivers her and in turn receives an unlikely deliverance in combat with his far more experienced opponent. It is he who now overcomes the lady's vow of chastity. For alas, without quite knowing why, she experiences maternal and erotic feelings for one who looks so much like her first and only beloved, her brother. She is not only grateful to him, she is proud of him. She ought to be taken aback by this fact, but she pays no attention to it. She has even been on the verge of recognizing the brocade of his garments as the very same material she sent along with the baby, but the connection eludes her conscious mind. And so the original sin is repeated, is raised to a higher power; the same mad pride of consanguinity emerges once again. For somewhere, in the depths of her body, in her animal instinct, she knew in spite of all her ignorance; nature within her does not resist, but insists. She herself later admits it; it rises into clarity: "But underneath, where truth abides in quietness, the identity had been known at first glance, and conscious-unconscious she had taken her own child for husband, because again he had been the only one equal in birth." And it was just the same with Gregorius, as he admits to her in the end, from the pinnacle of his holiness: "The measure of the sinfulness is controvertible before God, the more so that thy child, in that place where the soul makes no pretence, likewise very well knew that it was his mother whom he loved. . . . A youth

51

who sets out to find his mother and wins by conquest a wife who, however beautiful, could be his mother, must reckon with it that she might be his mother whom he marries. . . . But to his blood the identity of wife and mother was familiar long before he learned the truth. . . ."

This is the point where his personal sin begins, for he was born with the previous one. But should this sin really be called personal, since it takes place in the lower depths, over which man does not have full power? It is original sin, Christian original sin at any rate, and Adam's sin here merges with the specifically genealogical sin. In the same way Biblical man had to become man so that he must fall away from God—it is one and the same thing—and be redeemed by God's Grace, so it is here in the special case of Gregorius. He must be driven into an even deeper chasm of sin by marrying his mother and begetting two children who are his sisters. When he continues to brood over his unknown origins and the meddling of an inquisitive maid-servant brings the truth to light, what we have is a repetition to a still higher degree of what had happened before. The sinful son does not merely go on a knightly crusade like his father. Rather, he inflicts upon himself the ultimate and truly Christian penance: in beggar's robes, without even bread or bowl, with only the ominous ivory tablet inscribed with his story, he sets forth into the wilds where "only the heavens could be his roof-tree," into the moors, the trackless forest, and stubble fields that bruise his bare feet, with nothing to eat but leftovers given him by charcoal burners. And once more he comes to fisherfolk, and this time the rude jeering and hearty insults of the man of the house are balm to him, although the wife, moved by some premonition, intercedes on his behalf. He is allowed to sleep in the shed. And then once more he is cast on an island, though not this time an island with a guardian cloister, but a barren reef in the lake, totally unpeopled. What is more, he eagerly accepts the fisherman's sadistic suggestion that his feet should be chained by a leg-iron. But wasteland, ignominy, exposure, the life of an anchorite, are not yet penance enough. He must be driven to the utmost extreme, beyond human limits; he shrivels to an unrecognizable spiny creature not much bigger than a hedgehog, barely kept alive by a few drops of "earth milk" that ooze from the rock. This minimum of nourishment is the sign of Grace. Henceforth, even as he contracts physically, he grows spiritually. Two Roman dignitaries are instructed by visions to summon Gregorius to the newly vacant papal throne, and he is fetched back into human life through a series of events explicable only by his miraculous elevation into saintliness.

The penitent Sibylla makes a pilgrimage to the celebrated pope in the hope that in his holy wisdom he can set her mind at rest concerning the souls of her loved ones. There is a scene similar to the audience of old Jacob and the band of brothers with the exalted Joseph: a scene of recognition and reconciliation. The sinful child has become the Holy Father; child, husband, and father form a trinity. In the end, the two, "in love and grief, in repentance and grace," cannot be anything to each other but brother and sister in Christ—brother and sister in the spiritually purified sense that implies chastity. Events have come full circle. Providence has drawn its paradigm and completed its demonstration.

To be sure, this parable presents the element of the miraculous in its most exaggerated form. Here is the saintly legend at its most basic, in which utmost sin is transformed by utmost penance into utmost salvation. The circle of meaning, however humanized by the colorful, humorous "spirit of narrative," is traced with such precision, with such indomitable logic, that the story and its moral inevitably become caricature. And Thomas Mann would not be himself if he had foregone the opportunity to develop a situation to its limit, even a situation bordering on the burlesque. Nevertheless, at a deeper level the story wonderfully illuminates the spirit of Christian doctrine: incest represents the summit of human presumption, of racial pride and self-idolization, and as such can be equated with Adam's primal original sin against God and his fellow-men. It is original sin insofar as it is buried deep within the animal part of man and is not quite accessible to the personal will. It is, however, also personal sin because even in ignorance there is germinal knowledge and underneath naked instinct there lies a spark of will. No one can claim pure innocence, and yet no one is so completely guilty that Grace cannot bring salvation. Indeed, Grace actually longs for the mighty sinner with his shattering repentance.

If *The Holy Sinner* shows an extreme of genealogical narcissism, exaltation of selfhood, *Felix Krull* exemplifies an excessive passion for otherness. The hero is endowed with a hypertrophic imagination whose locus is his own body. Therefore it is readily capable of assuming tangible forms. Imagination originating in the body gives rise to rapid impersonation.

Krull is drawn into delinquency by his lack of specific gravity, his lack of an inhibiting selfhood, his "receptivity to the subtlest stimuli," combined with a talent for all too easily assuming other roles. He is certainly a swindler, but of a very special sort. And can he really be considered a criminal? Only in a very limited sense.

From beginning to end this "Felix" appears as a darling of the gods, a "favorite child of heaven," someone convinced of his own charm. Despite the prison term he alludes to, the old man who is penning the confessions still preserves his sense of happiness and faith in his good fortune. From the outset he is favored, or rather blessed, not only with physical attractions and charm, but also with the dangerous talent for self-transformation. He has a knack for imitation, simulation, disguise. He can mimic people's voices and ways of speaking as facilely as he can forge their handwritings. Underlying these accomplishments is a gift for observation, "perceiving," "extension of feeling," and thus a faculty for love-making, for intensifying and enlarging his being by taking in the broadest and most variegated possibilities. Moreover, he has the remarkable ability to control and shape those qualities on which the success, happiness, and good fortune of his life depend. Because he feels himself composed of "finer flesh and blood," he musters all his talents and virtuosity to provide real proof of his "election." For his active imagination would do him little good were it not for the instinct and good taste whereby he guides it, were it not for the generosity, aristocratic feeling, and occasionally the modesty with which he selects his opportunities. He brings to bear a good deal of disciplined effort —so much so that one might almost speak of responsibility. All these things are what distinguish him from a "common criminal."

To be sure, he commits thefts, he lies, impersonates. But aside from the childish forays into the *pays de Cocaigne* of the delicatessen—and "it was not alone their high quality [of the sweetmeats] that enchanted me; even more it was the carrying over of my dream treasures into my waking life that made up the sum of my delight . . ."—except for this incident, no one is ever a whit the worse off as a result of Krull's transgressions. Madame Houpflé's jewel case slips into Krull's suitcase by itself in the course of the customs inspection. Whatever profit he makes from its contents, as well as from the subsequent commanded robbery in her hotel room, is actually a gift from this half-motherly, masochistic lady novelist who has a passion for young men. All this comes about because Felix, boyishly shy and chivalrous on "grounds of taste," has refused to whip her as she requests. And the grandiose fraud of the aristocratic world tour which he later embarks on is not an affair of his own seeking, but is done as a favor to the young Marquis, whose role Krull casually agrees to assume. Felix even exchanges his own bank account for the Marquis' letter of credit. In concluding the agreement, he specifically forbids anyone to "presuppose something like cunning in me. Where cunning is concerned, I am quite useless. Cunning is not gentlemanly." Were it not that he really has gentlemanly qualities, he would be quite incapable of playing his role. He has already unhesitatingly rejected various tempting proposals made to him while he was still a waiter—by an infatuated English girl and a wealthy Scottish lord. Yet he declined these advantageous offers with the utmost consideration for the feelings of those concerned: "The main thing was that a confident instinct within me rebelled against a form of reality that was simply handed to me and was in addition sloppy—rebelled in favor of free play and dreams, self-created and self-sufficient, dependent, that is, only on the imagination. When as a child I had waked up determined to be an eighteen-year-old prince named Karl, and had then freely maintained this pure and enchanting conceit for as long as I wished—that had been the right thing for me. . . ." The point is that he cherishes freedom, and such freedom entails discipline.

Anyone who senses a great talent in himself longs to develop that talent creatively. Thus the boy Felix consciously practices the art of dissimulation, which stands him in good stead at his examination for military service; thus he delights in "dressing up," perfects his manners and accomplishments. Hailing cabs outside the theater is good training for the roles of elevator boy and waiter by which he will later mount into the upper reaches of society. All along, outside assistance flows toward him as if by magic, as always happens when any strong characterological trait manifests itself. He receives valuable education from his godfather Schimmelpreester, the carnival-loving painter who plays games of masquerade with Felix, as well as from the coarse prostitute Rosza, who puts him through a rigorous course in love. Krull feels keen enjoyment in practicing such arts and performing such roles. He enjoys playing on himself like an instrument. He enjoys the gentle transition from dream to reality, the haziness, the interchangeability of the two conditions, the "delicate hovering quality of his existence." He enjoys disguises even when they are humbling; but even more pleasurable is an ambiguous role, such as that of being a liftboy with a bank account. "And so, possessor of a checkbook though I was, I remained a liftboy. . . . There was a certain charm in playing this role against a background of secret wealth, thanks to which my becoming livery took on the quality of a costume. . . . My secret wealth transformed my uniform and my job into a role, a simple extension of my talent for 'dressing-up.' Although later on I achieved dazzling success in passing myself off for more than I was, I now passed myself off for less, and it is an open question which deception gave me the greater inner amusement, the greater delight in this fairytale magic."

If he is distinguished from the real criminal by these higher demands of the imagination, by his pleasure not only in life's crude material satisfactions but in airy, fastidious freedom, he is also distinguished from the professional impersonator, the actor, by the seriousness he brings to his metamorphoses: "It's not my custom to take life as a joke," he tells the Marquis whose identity he is to assume. ". . . Frivolity is not my style, especially in the matter of jokes; for certain jokes are pointless if they are not taken seriously. A good joke does not come off unless one approaches it with complete seriousness." This is why acting, for which his gifts might have destined him, does not meet his needs: in acting, the sphere of illusion is too sharply divided from reality. The actor uses his art of impersonation on alien, distant material—the greater the distance, the finer the art. Krull is his own material; his own reality is his material. He does not merely dissimulate, he does not merely counterfeit another role: he identifies with that other person, body and soul. His aim is not imposture but identity, confusingly free, dreamlike, and protean identity.

As a child Krull came face to face with the crass reality of the actor when his godfather took him to the theater and later dropped in on the dressing rooms. The boy was captivated by the splendor and sovereignty of the figure on the stage; he was all the more repelled by the real man behind the illusion. The opposite principle is exemplified by the circus performers whom he sees in Paris; as trapeze artists or clowns they commit their whole being to the act, to the point where they no longer have lives of their own. Felix Krull himself hovers between the two forms of existence, living "as a likeness" and yet really living. In serious-minded freedom he juggles with his lived life.

It is natural that a person as obsessed with transformation as Krull should be attracted and excited by the cosmic aspects of the question, as unfolded to him (while Krull is just setting out on his new aristocratic existence) by his table companion in the dining car, Professor Kuckuck. Kuckuck outlines the course of the world's evolutionary transformations and the ascent of one form into another, from existence to life to man. Krull learns that all forms are provisional, that life itself is but an episode.

All this accords with his own "praise of the transitory"[3] and "universal sympathy," his sense of the way things flow into one another and exert attraction on each other. The "vast expansiveness" of feeling which he acquires, thanks to this broad perspective, is closely akin to the erotic-sexual feeling which as a child he had named "The Great Joy." The strong impact of Kuckuck's lecture is reflected in the charming sermons Felix reads to Kuckuck's daughter, Zouzou, in Lisbon. Felix wants to convert the mocking, saucy girl to love. Hemmed in by the strict Latin conventions, the girl scorns and assails what repression denies her; she scoffs at love as "disgusting small-boy nastiness." And what Krull tells her, in fact almost sings to her—for he deliberately poeticizes love to counter the girl's foolish "crudeness"—is a theoretical glorification of love as that miracle of nature which succeeds "in wiping out the division between one person and the other." This miracle begins in the human eye and the intimacy of its gaze. This is a recurrent theme in the *Confessions*, and one which inspires some passages of moving beauty. (One is reminded of Werfel's poem *Blicke*, which similarly celebrates the power of the eye.) The eye is that "precious jelly made up of just such ordinary elements as the rest of creation, affirming like a precious stone that the elements count for nothing, but that imaginative and fortunate combination counts for everything . . . as long as the spark of life remains alert there, to throw such beautiful,

[3] The German title of a brief statement Thomas Mann wrote for a radio broadcast and published under the title of "Life Grows in the Soil of Time" in the *New York Herald Tribune*, October 27, 1952. Reprinted in *This I Believe*, edited by E. P. Morgan (New York: Simon and Schuster, 1952), pp. 113-14.

airy bridges across all the chasms of strangeness that lie between man and man." The miracle leads to the embrace and the kiss, which "is after all, pledge of that marvelous release from separateness and from the fastidious refusal to be interested in anything that is not oneself." "Only at the opposite poles of human contact, where there are no words or at least words no more, in the glance and the embrace, is happiness really to be found, for there also are unconditional freedom, secrecy, and profound ruthlessness." And the book might indeed end on this little hymnic speech which celebrates the "denial of the aversion of stranger for the stranger, a secret sign of omnipresent love." It is the metaphoric apotheosis of Felix Krull's passion for the *other*.

However, the *Confessions* do not end here; in fact they do not end with the episode or this one volume alone, but promise events to come. Events lead up to a real kiss, a triumphant test case, whereby the girl's inhibitions are put to flight. But that marks the end of the adventure with the nubile girl. The tender embrace is interrupted by the appearance of the mother, an imposing beauty who, with her majestic sensuality, commandeers and devours the young "Marquis' " love. This makes good sense and is totally welcome to Krull, for actually he had fallen in love with both together, the pretty daughter and the beautiful mother; what attracted him was the scintillating doubleness, the "combination"—in this case the mother and daughter, as back in his Frankfurt days he had been unforgettably struck by the sight of a brother and sister who briefly stepped out on the balcony of their hotel:

a reference, we might point out, to a remote but related sphere, the world of Gregorius.

In *The Holy Sinner* and in *Doctor Faustus*, even in *Joseph and his Brothers*, a particular paradox has been established: that grace proceeds to sin and sin to grace. In secular terms this means the blurring of the frontier between the impersonal and the person, between, on the one hand, inherited dispositions and circumstances, and, on the other, the will and accomplishments of the individual. In *Gregorius* the hand of Providence fulfills the same function that in *Faustus* is assumed by biological demonism—for the devil of *Faustus* was, after all, only an atavistic, theological projection of the inescapable law that evil is inextricably involved with the power of creation. Felix Krull gives much thought to the paradoxes of this problem: "Education is not won in dull toil and labor; rather it is the fruit of freedom and apparent idleness; one does not achieve it by exertion, one breathes it in; some secret machinery is at work to that end; a hidden industry of the senses and the spirit . . . is hourly active to promote it, and you could go so far as to say that one who is chosen learns even in his sleep. For one must after all be of educable stuff in order to be educated. No one grasps what he has not possessed from birth . . . and here again it is very hard to draw a just and clear distinction between personal desert and what are called favorable circumstances. . . ." But there are times when Felix considers the question from the opposite angle: "Was it not very difficult to make a sharp distinction between natural deserts and moral? . . . Was it true that I had had so little to do, in an inner sense, with those assets? Had I not instead the unmistakable assurance that they were my own work to a significant degree, and that my voice might easily have turned out common, my eyes dull, my legs crooked, had my soul been less watchful." Here the natural graces are represented as a product of moral qualities.

The same paradox is present in the relationship between freedom and discipline: freedom is preserved only through discipline, but initial freedom is required to make discipline possible. Though Felix Krull is so talented and trained for love's pleasures, "the extraordinary demands" imposed on his energies forbid him to squander himself "in enervating passion." And yet he holds that it is "the enervating that benerves us—if vital prerequisites are met —and makes us capable of performances and enjoyments in the world that are beyond the compass of the un-benerved."

These intricate and varied paradoxes are the motive force of Krull's whole existence; in fact, they are the very substance of this improbable existence, in which dream and reality, truth and deception, all but merge. Here the very truth is elusive mutability, transformation of identity, olympian manipulation of identity. In this graceful, deceptively easy book Thomas Mann has once more given us a picture of the artist, this time of an artist who works with his own flesh and blood.

1955

Translated from the German by Krishna and Richard Winston.

REPRESENTATION AND
REVOLUTION

THAT master of the art of narration whose memory we are honoring was the last major exponent of the great changeover from the nineteenth to the twentieth century. This was no ordinary case of one cultural era giving way to another, but an unprecedented and fundamental shift that called everything we possessed into question, and rocked the ground under our feet. I would also venture that among the other major figures of the time—André Gide, Paul Valéry, Marcel Proust, James Joyce, Franz Kafka, Stefan George, Rainer Maria Rilke, Hugo von Hofmannsthal, August Strindberg, Frank Wedekind, George Bernard Shaw—there was none who represented this radical shift so fully, with greater range in time and space, as Thomas Mann.

He himself once said that he never felt himself meant for the role of the exiled resistance fighter, the oppositionist and agitator, but rather for the role of representor. As he saw it, his task was to portray the essence, the quintessential spirit of his nation, Germany—embodied, to be sure, in the present historical moment, along with all its questions and doubts (for how else could one represent this most problematical of peoples?). But *representation* it was, in the sense of a sublimation of nationalism, and thus it was an essentially conservative position. Yet since he was an artist, drawn irresistibly into the search for truth—drawn, that is, into the heart of things—and since he lived in such harrowed and convulsive times as ours, he was not destined to represent stability and conservatism. He was thrust into another sort of representation, wider in scope and importance, more complex and more perilous: representation of the great transition in which we are caught up. This type of representation was of necessity revolutionary in character, and led inexorably to a revolution in literary forms and motifs. To represent such a cataclysmic period could not be anything less than revolutionary. In spite of strong psychological resistance, Thomas Mann was forced by inward and outward circumstances to undertake this revolutionary representation, and in the end he carried out his stupendous task as no other could.

All the other great writers I have mentioned describe a limited period, a partial current, or a special strand of reality. Thomas Mann alone, in his career and in the range of his works, managed to grasp the whole, so far as that is humanly possible. This is a simple fact, and does not involve judgment of the relative worth of the others; it is pointless to be assigning ranks to minds of this caliber. One excellence often cancels or makes up for another. A more limited field of vision, or a more homogeneous view, may enable some writers to achieve more clarity, more intensity, indeed may offer more consolation. But the writer who is obliged to feel and to set forth the full inescapable tragedy, the total overturning of life as we know it, is compelled to certain sacrifices.

I believe that one cannot do full justice to Thomas

Mann's work unless one views it in this light, unless one sees it as the mighty testimony of a man who experienced both within himself and outside himself all the enormous dichotomies and dilemmas, all the conflicts and paradoxes, all the hellish and demonic phenomena of our times. He did experience them, and in the course of describing them he descended into often very treacherous depths. He asked his questions fearlessly and unsparingly —all his life he asked and raised questions, and to temper these sometimes terrible questions he could only keep them at a distance, taking a position that seemed to declare: all these things are human, and in the midst of their horror are sometimes amusing, soothingly amusing. Let us not lose sight of that.

In his early essay, *Bilse and I* (written as a *pro domo* piece in 1906), "an open letter and small manifesto," Thomas Mann speaks of the work of the artist and what he himself has discovered about such work. Along with the artist's joy and pride, there is a cry of pain. For not only is it given to the poet to "express what he suffers" —in the words of Goethe's *Tasso*—he must also suffer what he expresses. "The artist," the essay states, "pursues insight and form: deep insight and beautiful form, and what gives his life its moral consecration is his patient endurance of the pain that is inseparable from his two goals. Do people understand about this pain? That all forming, creating, producing means pain, struggle and travail. . . . This should be generally known. But the fact that insight, the artistic insight generally referred to as 'observation' is also painful—is that also known? Observation as passion, martyrdom, heroism—who knows of this? . . . Let no one imagine . . . that the refinement and alertness of the observing sensibility can reach an extraordinary pitch without there also being an increase in the capacity for suffering. This capacity can reach such a degree that all experience becomes suffering. . . ." This agonizing sensibility, described here as a characteristic common to all artists, has reached special heights in our century. Among its victims, Marcel Proust, Rilke, and Virginia Woolf were the most extreme. If one considers what Thomas Mann, that very German artist, had in his field of vision in the course of his lifetime, what he had to try to understand and give artistic shape to, it becomes clear what his irony means. His way of parodying and caricaturing the most serious phenomena is not mere levity but a weapon, a strategy for keeping experience off his back, for keeping it in bounds, in proportion and in perspective, for gaining mastery over it. It is no accident that the crucial works of modern fiction, the works of Joyce, Gide, Valéry, Kafka, Sartre, Musil, and Broch, all manifest various brands of irony, as either the basic or an auxiliary ingredient. The writer instinctively resorts to irony as a means to endure the experiences of our time.

With Thomas Mann the irony is perfectly open; he uses it explicitly and in manifold variations. The particular tension that characterizes this artistic stance is the stylistic expression of the many tensions present in Mann's experience. I would suggest that Thomas Mann is very much the man of tensions—the far-flung extensions and powerful tensions inherent in his own disposition and fate as well as in his world and era. I have mentioned the first, all-encompassing tension between *representation and revolution*. It was inherent, as I have already indicated, in the historical extension of Thomas Mann's own life-span over a period of epochal upheavals. From beginning to end he pondered and described the multiplicity and monstrosity of his transitional age in the metaphoric, indeed parabolic, disguise of his fiction and in the direct analysis of his essays. It is all recorded in his writings, as even the phenomenon of a consciously lived historical span is delineated in his lecture *Meine Zeit* ("The Years of My Life").

What a far cry from bourgeois stability, from the strictly circumscribed, nationally and occupationally hedged-in order of the Bismarckian world to the wide open, storm-swept universal wilderness which is our world, one in which all physical boundaries have in fact been eliminated, no matter how much people still wrangle over them; in which the real issue has become the global overthrow of all existing orders, external and internal! What a long way from the sturdy "solidity and propriety" of the legendary gold currency and "blue chip investments," and Fontane's picture of a society where conventionality is as yet barely touched by the frost of uncertainty—to a situation in which, as Ernst Jünger puts it, "technics and ethics have become curiously synonymous"! What a long way from gas lanterns and horse-drawn trolleys to neon lights and jet aircraft! What a mighty stylistic transformation from realism and naturalism to structuralism and surrealism! What a long way, in short, from *Buddenbrooks* to *Doctor Faustus*! The decisive turning points on this long road are *The Magic*

Mountain and *Reflections of a Non-political Man,* both written under the impact of the first great world war.

Added to the contrasts resulting from this long time span is the celebrated inborn *tension between the burgher and the artist,* which is again essentially the stress between representor and revolutionary. This conflict was the original problem, the "primal experience" that laid the groundwork for the far-reaching and considerably graver human issues Thomas Mann was later to deal with. Only in an intact bourgeois world could the problem be posed as clearly and simply as it was to the young Thomas Mann. But the world of the burgher, the world of secure normality went to smash; the great maelstrom of values was set into motion. And from the Tonio Kröger of Lübeck and Munich to that cosmic Tonio Kröger, Adrian Leverkühn, the original conflict spread in ever-widening rings, encircling the tremendous tensions that had meanwhile developed outside in the world and within the artist himself. Thus the polar opposites crossed each other and merged, and in turn underwent internal divisions; plus and minus were reversed; the significance of the poles was changed, inverted, developed, enriched; and in the course of this self-proliferating questioning, of this constant re-examination, the three-dimensional picture, the complex image of our human situation, took the shape it wears in Mann's later works. In spite of all these profound changes it is one consistent process; and I could scarcely name another author whose entire work reveals such pervasive inner unity, yielding such a coherent, logically unfolding whole. This entire process took place under the cover of narration so that the wealth of novelistic detail might easily make one overlook the fierce desire for understanding which was the fundamental and innermost motive for all of Mann's artistic endeavor.

The contrast between the burgher and the artist, between normal, sheltered existence and unusual or supra-normal existence, permeates the whole of Mann's early work, not just *Tonio Kröger* but the other novels of this period and the first theoretical writings as well. It also appears under various guises in *Buddenbrooks*: when spiritual turmoil and reflectiveness break into Senator Buddenbrook's traditional-hallowed sober formality; or when the appearance of artistic impulses in the last remaining heir, Hanno, signalizes the downfall of this bourgeois line. We recall that moving episode when the Senator sits for hours in his garden pavilion absorbed in Schopenhauer, never looking up, never changing his position. He has suddenly become aware of the consolation to be found in ideas which answer the need long burning within him. A world has been revealed to him, the world of the mind, and he makes a valiant effort to hold it, to remain in it. Paradoxically, this world restores his hope for a transcendent return to normal, a condition he had lost with the failing of his powers: a return to normal after death, through the dissolution of the self. And this weakened burgher already feels quite like the artist Tonio Kröger: "Have I ever hated life—pure, strong, relentless life? Folly and misconception! I have but hated myself, because I could not bear it. I love you, I love you all, you blessed, and soon, soon, I shall cease to be cut off from you by all the narrow bonds of myself; soon will that in

me which loves you be free and be in and with you
—in and with you all." What a curious involution we already have here: that spirituality becomes the instrument
of the burgher's longing.

But the antinomy between burgher and artist contains
another, more far-reaching one: the *antinomy between
life and work*. In the study *The Hungry*, a sketch or
preliminary exercise which in many ways anticipates
Tonio Kröger, we are shown a writer watching a carni-
val party from the sidelines (like Tonio Kröger at his
dancing lessons and later at the dance in the Danish sea-
side resort): "Ah, to be not an artist but a man, if only
once, if only on a night like this! If only once to escape
the inexorable doom which rang in his ears: 'You may not
live, you must create; you may not love, you must
know!'" And when he leaves the theater and steps out
into the street, from the hollow-cheeked face of a ragged
outcast stares the reflection of his own bitter longing,
directed at *him* for his air of prosperity and well-being.
The paradox of the situation strikes him: "My God,
what an error, what a crass misunderstanding. . . . But
we are brothers!" But this is not the end of the insight.
A question forms in his mind, a terrible doubt in which
further questions lurk: "Wrong! All wrong! And as this
pity wholly filled him, he felt kindled somewhere deep
within an intuition at once painful and sweet. . . . Is he
the only one who errs? Where is the end of error? Is not
all longing on earth an error, this of mine first of all,
which craves the simple and the instinctive, dumb like itself, ignorant of the enlightenment which comes through
mind and art, the release through the Word?"

It was indeed an error. And here we find the point of transition to the next phase of the complex problem: the answer is given in *Death in Venice*, where life reveals its demonic depths; in *The Magic Mountain*, where normal life dissolves into war, death, and misery; and in the *Joseph* novels, where the spirit rises from the "slime" of archaic instinctuality. But what is the answer? Only greater, more far-reaching questions.

For the positions are no longer so clearly defined. In *Death in Venice* we see for the first time how the unambiguous pairs of opposites begin to divide up. This story takes place inside the very world of art. And art appears here as a combination of two opposed elements. The actual *artistic* element consists in a disciplined, conscious mastery of material, and manifests itself in Gustav Aschenbach in character traits stemming from his Prussian ancestry. These are precisely what have enabled Aschenbach to achieve his solid and respectable reputation, his position as official preceptor and representor. In contrast, there is the other, specifically *poetic* element, the Dionysian, ecstatic, magical temperament which instead of imposing form on beauty rapturously surrenders to beauty. There can be no true work of art without these transports also, no true artist without this capacity for abandonment. How do the positions line up here? On the one hand the artist seems to coincide with the correct burgher, while the poet, yielding unrestrainedly to his longing for the beautiful, seems to coincide with earlier, romantic artists. On the other hand, Aschenbach at his peak was an ascetic who held himself aloof from life; when he becomes an ecstatic, a lover, he throws himself into the arms of life, but life sweeps him on to disease and death. It is not only art that here reveals its complexity; life too has become ambivalent. Whereas life earlier was equated with harmless bourgeois normality, happiness, the "bliss of the commonplace," a realm inaccessible to the artist because there was simply no way of entering it, life now reveals its secret abysses and proves to be the source of demonic forces which drag the artist into a deadly whirlpool. As in *The Magic Mountain*, life and death are no longer clearly separated from one another. One can see clearly how the issues are proliferating and becoming increasingly complicated.

In *Doctor Faustus* the fundamental opposition spreads out into ever-broadening implications. The conflict is no longer confined to a narrow, local present; rather it moves in a cosmic space that arches in a great vault over the ages. Here the artist stands for the *universal man of mind* and the burgher is widened and deepened into *humanity in general*. The Faustian artist must obey the old prohibition: "You may not live, you must create; you may not love, you must know!" But here the iron law acquires a bearing far beyond the merely personal. For this book deals with the tragic alienation of the man of mind—tragic not only for him but for the very destiny of man. Kröger's yearning for Inge and Hans has not disappeared, but it has been transformed into the equally shy, secret, despairing yearning of the genius for an intimate relationship with humanity. And if Hans and Inge could contentedly pursue their happy blond lives without paying any heed to Tonio—for they no doubt were happier without him—the same cannot be said for humanity.

Humanity cannot remain unaffected when it is completely cut off from its own highest consciousness, from knowledge and conscience. Humanity no longer consists of the innocuously normal and politically untroubled world of the burgher; rather it is a turbulent, directionless mass which has had commerce with fearful demons. And, after all, has not the artist, with his uncompromising and defiant purity, his total dedication to his search, his innovations, and his own perfection, succumbed to a demon; has he not, with his fierce artistic discipline, incurred vast guilt in the face of humanity? In Aschenbach this artistic discipline still represented an identifiable common sentiment. But now it leaves the sphere of human warmth far behind to follow the lonely imperatives of its abstract course. Here again, in the artist as in humanity, demonic forces are at work.

These are the new and ultimate issues. They first emerged out of the social upheavals of the First World War, when political and moral tensions of world import forced their way into Mann's own inner conflicts. To be sure, these concepts developed over several decades. The turning points, as I have remarked, occur on the one hand in the *Reflections of a Non-Political Man*, where Thomas Mann slowly and painfully struggles free of his former convictions, and where all fixed conceptions turn fluid in the heat of polemics; and on the other hand in *The Magic Mountain*, which is Mann's great reckoning with the pre-war world and his analysis of the various political and moral attitudes that passed on into the new world. The old times are over, the insular days of illusory European peace which was long ago undermined by hidden currents. The new age has arrived, and with it wars and cataclysms and turbulence, both on the surface and in the depths.

For Thomas Mann the detachments were difficult; they were always—and this is to his honor—the result of long and searching processes from which he not infrequently came out worsted. Often he arrived at his conclusions at the wrong moment. In the midst of the revolutionary chaos of 1918 he was still desperately defending his inherited patrician, conservative convictions, his dream of representing German culture. In 1932, in the face of the gathering onslaught of Nazism, he publicly raised his voice in favor of democracy, internationalism, and conciliation. This was his first step toward exile, toward the break with his homeland. But this break did not come easily to him either. Even in exile he was long reluctant to abandon those among the German people who were still faithful to him, to cut them loose from any public bond with him. It was only the most brazen crimes on the part of the Nazis which drove him to militant opposition and produced that outrage of all his human feelings—which was a long time subsiding, once the war was over.

It is both unfair and naïve to brand these changes as inconsistencies. Unfortunately they have often been so branded on both sides of the ocean. There was basically only one change, a difficult, painful evolution, a growth of insight and experience in accord with the times. This change was simply the dynamic expression of the permanent tension in Mann's being, a redistribution of the forces constituting that tension. From start to finish he remained both a burgher and an artist. And just as his works in the years before 1914 reveal no trace of the stuffy, airless petit bourgeois quality of the parochial German nationalism then prevalent, so his later attitudes and work never lack evidence of his profound craving for form and manners, for discipline and principle. In his early writings dangerous demonic forces are already churning beneath the surface of his essentially traditional narrative method. These forces, intellectual and sensual temptations displaced from life into art, are not given free rein until much later. Yet in Mann's late works the most daring things are presented in a faultless form and manner, as indeed Mann in his outward life and appearance always maintained a patrician bearing. He was always both conservative and radical, thoroughly proper and deeply demonic, even diabolical at times—how else could he have understood the devil so well? He filled his part as representor, was avid for this public role, yet was tormented by its problems. He was cosmopolitan, human—and with all this, exceedingly German. All these tensions were always present within him; at the beginning one aspect was more in evidence; later, growing experience and insight brought the other more to the fore. Christian Buddenbrook, the decadent scapegrace who is nevertheless a brilliant story-teller, is bothered by a hallucination: "You come into your room when it is getting dark and see a man sitting on the sofa nod to you when there is no man there." Here, tucked into the first novel of the twenty-five-year-old writer, is the precursor of the figure who will determine the fate of the seventy-year-old writer's Adrian Leverkühn, with whom he will engage in a final accounting on the life of the artist.

Tensions such as these are the basic structural elements of the great novels, *The Magic Mountain,* the *Joseph* tetralogy, *Doctor Faustus.* Let us not forget that these books are not mere literature; they are fragments of life, embodying the struggle to live and to know of a man who experienced broadly and deeply, who was insatiable, Faustian, intellectually audacious, willing to go to extremes, and who was aware of the mystery of reality and the magic power of the Word.

The central tension of Thomas Mann, and perhaps all the tensions of his life and thought, are reflected in his intense relationship to the two founding fathers of German literature, Goethe and Schiller—mutually exclusive literary ancestors, one would have thought. Goethe, of course, was the model and prototype by whom he measured himself and in whose spirit he steeped himself. Mann found in Goethe the two impulses which were also at work in himself: the subterranean volcanic forces of the demonic, held in check by a commanding and majestic power of representation gained through balance and resignation. A certain deliberate composure, an imperturbable stateliness of Mann's prose, which in fact is usually ironically overstressed, derives from Goethe's prose manner. This manner has in fact left its mark upon the most varied temperaments up to this day, more often obstructing authentic expression than favoring it. We feel this influence in Stifter and Gottfried Keller; it is present in Hofmannsthal, Borchardt, Schröder, and even Carossa, and its various permutations would be well worth study.

If Goethe was for Thomas Mann the paradigm of serene, all-embracing superiority, exemplar of the highest representation, what impressed him in Schiller was the dynamic and revolutionary aspect, the ever-greater tension of will, which is at times strained beyond its own capacities, the continuous industry and "creative self-denial," the *motus animi continuus*. He valued Schiller's propensity for deep thought, his passionate speculation, his sensitive concern for the state of the world; and last but not least his resolute battle for the freedom and dignity of man. These qualities were all in Thomas Mann's character, and long before his memorial lecture there are early statements and the story, *A Weary Hour*, that show his sympathetic affinity, even his love, for this conqueror of all base obstacles, this true hero of life. There is something deeply moving in the fact that the memorial lecture on Schiller should have been the last major work Mann completed, so that in effect it formed the epilogue to his own life.

In keeping with these two strong and basically divergent influences, Mann's artistic style reveals an unusual combination of *dynamic* and *static characteristics, a musical vein* and *a visual vein*. Music is for him—as it was not for Goethe—the most congenial of the arts. Music, far more than the plastic arts, corresponds with his way of feeling. But what attracts him about music is not so much its flowing, rushing, swelling element, not its melodic and symphonic qualities as such, nor is it essentially the romantic power to compel self-surrender. What attracts him to music is the artistic work in music, its capacity to bind together and structure what would otherwise pour itself out formlessly. He feels music to be the sublime borderline art in which auditory sensation becomes visual. As he formulates it in the *Reflections of a Non-Political Man*, music is "art as sounding ethics . . . as fugue and *punctum contra punctum* . . . a semi-sacred structure in which each detail interacts with others, meaningfully, intelligently, bound without mortar and held together 'by the Hand of God.' . . ." This kind of *art pour l'art*, he explains, is precisely his esthetic ideal and one which we can clearly discern in his works of fiction.

What pure dynamics, melody, and harmony are for music, the purely narrative element is for prose. Indeed, the majority of readers are more or less intoxicated by the so-called story, even as the average listener succumbs to the intoxication of musical melody. To be sure, the comparison between music and any piece of writing can have only limited validity; for writing is a combination of tonal and visual elements, and narrative in particular achieves its magical effect chiefly from that intense precision of description which comes from seeing, from observation. Thomas Mann is an enchanting story-teller— what characters, atmospheres, and milieus he has conjured up and made everlasting for us! Whether he is describing a railway accident or a spiritistic séance, a medical examination at an induction center, or a tournament, a bullfight, or Christmas in the Buddenbrook household, the Swiss Alps or the Egyptian city of cats, Venice or the unpeopled wilds of India, the delightful hermit of that wilderness or Madame Houpflé, Mager the headwaiter at the inn Zum Elephanten in Weimar, or even Goethe himself—Mann is always totally immersed in what he is presenting, and his passionate absorption in the events, the character, the state of mind draws us into the story and will not let us go. He deeply reveled in the painful delight of narration and creative observation and could so well induce that intoxication with mere "story," that readers are often tempted to forget the other, *artistic* element in his works, their real meaning, for which the narrative splendors are only window-dressing. He never tells a story for its own sake. But when this significance is developed in discussions or technical disquisitions, some readers, forever hungry for interesting occurrences, are disappointed. They fail to realize that what they incline to reject as an alien element is not only artistically legitimate but also forms a part, and a very essential part, of the story itself. For we no longer live in a world in which the important things take place picturesquely in the midst of natural human conditions. We live in a world in which what is originally given us already belongs largely to the rational, technical sphere. The decisive raw material of reality nowadays resides in discussions, investigations, and technical processes. Thomas Mann recognized and acted upon this fact. That is his bold innovation and must be counted one of the revolutionary advances of modern fiction.

The dynamism of the narrative thus always appears in Mann tamed, mastered, and symbolically illuminated by the strict meaningfulness of structure. And to read his books correctly one must study them as one studies the score of a strictly structured musical work of art; he himself used the term "score" for his own work.

Let me point out, finally, a further tension to be found

in Mann's work and in his attitude toward the world. Mann's eightieth birthday was celebrated, as was proper to a career which grew increasingly brilliant far into old age, like the jubilee in the reign of a great sovereign. Yet amidst the chorus of extravagant praise there were occasional allusions to some essential lack in Mann's work: the otherworldly spiritual element, some principle of guidance, some basis for values. Thus, for example, reference would be made to other great figures who have, as the phrase went, "erected lofty spiritual edifices of thought." The reproach, as expressed by a German writer of the younger generation, Hans Egon Holthusen, was that Mann presented "a world without transcendence." I think it important to discuss this allegation and attempt to clarify the issue.

It is quite true that Mann's work deals with *this* world, our erratic and erring, discordant and highly dubious world, a world in which the problems, of which every age has had its ample share, have suddenly become so virulent and urgent as to imperil the very fact of man's continuance without losing his humanity, his age-old human qualities. Thomas Mann's works are, as I have said, questions, and they all end with questions. They probe into our human condition; they are concerned with gaining insight and understanding. And they strive for the most extreme, unsparing truthfulness. I believe we cannot penetrate and overcome the chaotic situation we are in without such ruthless investigation. Of the major writers who have taught us to see the deeper reality of our world —Gide, Joyce, Kafka, Valéry, Faulkner, even Ernst Jünger in his better moments—who was capable of giving us un-

ambiguous, clearly defined values? They could not pur-
vey what they did not have. Their artistic duty, as they
saw it, was first of all to depict things as they are and
through this depiction perhaps to reach a point where a
new directive could be posted. This was an honest ap-
proach. On the other hand, what help to us, here and
now is Heidegger's absolute "supra-existent" being?
What help is the theoretical freedom postulated by the
French existentialists? It is comparatively not so difficult
to envision worlds that hold themselves above the challenge of reality, beautiful, highly cultivated, morally edi-
fying universes, enclaves, islands within our poor, tortured
world, or spiritual havens up among the clouds. Insofar
as such worlds are religious, let us not say a word against
them. But however comforting they may be, they represent an escape, a flight from our painful reality. Besides,
Mann's critics are wrong to equate transcendence with
otherworldliness. There is an earthly transcendence, an
immanent transcendence, the transcendence of the mind,
and Mann's works are permeated through and through
with this transcendence.

With respect to values, Mann's critics overlook almost
half of his opus, the theoretical, directly cognitive half.
This is an integral part of his production, as important
as his artistic creations. These two aspects of his work are,
in fact, very closely related to each other. They accom-
pany each other, interpret each other, and sometimes seem
to contradict each other on many points. Between them,
too, there is tension. But on closer analysis one sees that
here as throughout the creative tension of his being, contradiction becomes counterpoint. If the principal aim of

the artistic works is understanding, the aim of the theoretical works is taking a stand. If the works of fiction consist of constant questioning, probing, search for insight, description, disclosure of the ambivalences and paradoxes into which our life has stumbled, the theoretical writings take one fundamental value, raise it to a postulate, and present it again and again, from all angles and in all variations, with indignant energy and passion. For if Thomas Mann was ever intemperate, it was in defense of this fundamental value. This value is the dignity of man. Mann's real, deeply committed fighting faith in the cause of man, in the cause of the humane—which in our time becomes the cause of peace and a faith in the possibility of pacifying our terrible conflicts—underlies all his theoretical works which, by the way, were often manifestos of the most active sort. And these manifestos throw light on the final intention of Mann's artistic endeavors. There also the central concern is man's fate.

I have said that Thomas Mann's novels are queries. All his life he continued asking questions, ever broader, more penetrating questions. But the answers evaded him. This wretched world of ours caused him great suffering and anxiety; I can personally attest to that. One of the most moving pieces he ever wrote unmistakably reveals his concern. It is almost his last, a study of Chekhov written shortly before the essay on Schiller. In it Mann quotes Chekhov's *A Tedious Story*, in which a famous and much honored old scholar must answer a question put to him in an hour of utter despair and hopelessness by his beloved foster child, a young actress. She is named Katia—like Thomas Mann's wife—and she asks: "What shall I do?

Just one word, Nicolai Stepanytch, I implore you, what shall I do?" And the learned old man can only answer: "I don't know; upon my honor and conscience, Katia, I don't know." And Thomas Mann goes on to quote Chekhov's bitter self-accusation: "We only picture life as it is and do not go one step further. . . . As things stand, the life of the artist has no point, and the more talented he is, the stranger and more incomprehensible his role becomes, because he is obviously working to amuse a foul beast of prey, and by so doing helping to support the existing order." "This existing order," Mann adds, "consisted of the unbearable conditions in the Russia of the 1890's under which Chekhov lived. But his distress, his doubts about the value of his work, his feeling for the strangeness and incomprehensibility of his role as an artist, such doubts are timeless and not confined to conditions prevailing in Russia at the end of the nineteenth century. . . . Chekhov has fellow sufferers today, writers who do not feel at ease with their fame either, because they are amusing a forlorn world without offering it a scrap of saving truth . . . writers who could not tell you the meaning of their work, and yet go on working, working to the very end."

The question of the role of the artist and of art within the social process has been a deeply personal concern of Thomas Mann throughout his life. But in this essay he arrives at its ultimate and somehow ethical formulation. The comforting meaning of his life's work now appears to him to lie within that work itself. As he said of Chekhov, "There is a connection between the growing mastery of form and his growing sensitivity toward the social evils of his time—in other words, his deepening awareness of what is condemned by society and dying, as well as that which is to come; in short, the connection between the aesthetic and the ethical. . . . Is it not this," Thomas Mann asks, "that gives the work of art its dignity, its meaning, its purpose? . . . To be sure, to poor Katia's question, 'What am I to do?' we have no other answer than 'Upon my honor and conscience, I don't know.' Nevertheless one goes on working, telling stories, giving form to truth, thereby entertaining a forlorn world and hoping darkly, sometimes almost confidently, that truth and serene form will avail to set free the human spirit and prepare mankind for a better, lovelier, worthier life."

1956

Translated from the German by Krishna and Richard Winston.

DOCTOR FAUSTUS FROM
ADAM TO SARTRE

THE figure of Doctor Faustus has had a long and colorful history, for of all the human prototypes he has been the one most provocative to the Western imagination. Indeed, together with Don Quixote and Don Juan—to both of whom he is closely related—Doctor Faustus has, in the course of recent centuries, become a symbol of Western man. Each of these three figures embodies the endless striving of modern man, his overstepping the limits of a bounded world in quest of adventure, his pursuit of the unknown which lures him into ever wider, ever more precarious ranges of experience, even farther and farther away from the good earth. Don Quixote is carried away by his romantic imagination; Don Juan, though he is commonly seen as a kind of carefree playboy, a lady-killer and libertine, is actually a very serious, indeed a tragic figure. Whether one sees in him the personification of man's insatiable drive, or the humanized Devil, as pictured by Otto Rank, or the seeker of the inexhaustibly new—he is the great transgressor, the breaker of human boundaries. He is in fact quite incapable of love; he is unable even to settle down to the enjoyment of erotic pleasures, but must conquer for the sake of conquest, goaded by a voracity for ever new and novel experience; and what eventually carries him down to Hell is the hubris of his excessive appetite.

Doctor Faustus comprehends the aspirations of both

Don Quixote and Don Juan, but fuses and broadens them into a more general endeavor. Adventure and conquest transcend the human sphere and reach out into cosmic realms. Even the erotic transgressions assume a metaphysical and cosmic cast.

I propose to give a brief account of the history of this chimeric Doctor Faustus, in whom historical events and persons are blended with mythical elements and spiritual implications. I want to trace this story in its various transfigurations from its origins to the modern era, in which it has revealed its powerful symbolic capacity for representing the character of Western man, indeed man as a whole. As such a symbol, it has served the needs of three artists highly representative of our own age: Thomas Mann, Paul Valéry, Jean-Paul Sartre. Indeed each of them, like Goethe before them, has used the Faustus story as a personal confession. Camus too planned a Faustus version, but unfortunately did not live to write it.

The story begins even before its actual beginnings. It begins with the myth of man's genesis. It begins with Adam. In the second and third chapters of Genesis we read: "And the Lord God commanded the man saying, Of every tree of the garden thou mayest freely eat: But of the tree of knowledge of good and evil, thou shalt not eat of it: for in the day that thou eatest thereof thou shalt surely die. . . . Now the serpent [this must be considered as the first appearance of the diabolic seducer—Goethe's Mephistopheles refers to it as 'my celebrated cousin'] . . . more subtle than any beast of the field which the Lord God had made . . . said unto the woman: Yea, hath God said, Ye shall not eat of every tree of the garden? And the woman said. . . . We may eat of the fruit of the trees of the garden: But of the fruit of the tree which is in the midst of the garden, God hath said, Ye shall not eat of it, neither shall ye touch it, lest ye die. And the serpent said unto the woman, Ye shall not surely die. For God doth know that in the day ye eat thereof, then your eyes shall be opened, and ye shall be as gods, knowing good and evil." And in fact when they did eat of it their eyes opened and human consciousness was born. With it came freedom of choice, shame, and labor. We have here the actual creation of man, the beginning of the human tragedy, of the human paradox. In his quest for godlike powers, man brought upon himself death and mortality. He invited suffering, strife, and crime.

It all started in the woman, the instrument and incarnation of all temptation, but in the man it was brought to its heights. Hence, the basic Christian sin has been hubris, man's arrogant transgression of his boundaries. And yet, it is precisely this which is the essential human quality, the very characteristic of the human being. "And the Lord God said, Behold, the man is become as one of us . . . and now, lest he put forth his hand, and take also of the tree of life. . . . Therefore the Lord God sent him forth from the Garden of Eden." "To put forth his hand . . . and take of the tree of life": no less than this is what man is trying to do today.

We have parallels of the biblical story in the Greek myths of Prometheus and Icarus. They too are ancestors of Doctor Faustus. Prometheus combines features present in the stories of both the magic-working doctor and his

counterpart the Devil. Prometheus, the rebel and champion of the mortals, endowed, as his name itself indicates,
with prophetic insight, stole fire from Olympus, thereby
incurring a truly infernal punishment. Chained to a rock
he was left to the mercy of an eagle that by day fed on
his liver, which in turn regenerated each night. According
to a later version of the myth, Zeus flung Prometheus
into Tartarus. Moreover, Prometheus had originally been
an attendant of Zeus and had fought on his side in the
war against the Titans. In this respect, he strikingly resembled Shamael (Hebrew, "Poison-demon"), the fallen
archangel of the Hebrews and the prototype of the Devil,
Satan (Hebrew, "the Obstructor").

It is noteworthy that throughout the ages the Devil was
seen as "the master of fire." Like Prometheus there are
also resemblances to Hephaistos, the divine blacksmith,
who was hurled down from Olympus and with whom
the Devil shares the afflictions of lameness and limping.
Thus we find that the figure of Prometheus contains both
protagonists of the Faustus story: the mortal, transgressing his God-imposed limits, and the god (or demigod)
forfeiting his status through an act of revolt. In each case
the punishment is perpetual torture and Inferno. Characteristically, Goethe in his early, "titanic" period, hesitated
between a Prometheus and a Faustus project.

Another prefiguration of the Faustian aspiration was
Icarus, who flew too high with his waxen wings, and
thereby also ventured into a forbidden suprahuman sphere
where the sun melted his wings so that he plummeted
into the sea. References to this exploit, the desire to soar,
to extend man's sway into the skies, indeed into Heaven,

the magical practice of flying—all this has become a prevalent feature of Faustus literature. Marlowe's chorus, in the prologue to his Faustus tragedy, compares Faustus to Icarus. Goethe's Faust, on his Easter walk with Wagner, voices Icarian sentiments:

> *Betrachte, wie in Abendsonnenglut*
> *Die grünumgebnen Hütten schimmern!*
> *Sie rückt und weicht, der Tag ist überlebt,*
> *Dort eilt sie hin und fördert neues Leben.*
> *O dass kein Flügel mich vom Boden hebt*
> *Ihr nach und immer nach zu streben!*

> Look how the cottages on the green
> Shine in the glow of the evening sun!
> He backs away, gives way, the day is overspent,
> He hurries off to foster life elsewhere.
> Would I could press on his trail, on his trail forever—
> Alas that I have no wings to raise me into the air![1]

And in the second part of Goethe's *Faust*, in the Euphorion episode (Euphorion is the son of Faust and Helena), the venturesome boy who leaps to his death not only presages Faustus' own fate but is a symbol for the rise of poetry, of romanticism, and, more particularly, Lord Byron's dying for the liberation of Greece.

The Icarian motif as expressed in images of flight fused in the Faustus stories with miraculous ascents into Heaven of heroes, prophets, and saintly men. Vestiges of these aerial travels—since all saintly attributes were appropriated by the sorcerers—were the various flight motifs of

---

[1] Translated by Louis MacNeice.

demonology: witches' broomsticks, magic cloaks and winged steeds, flying fairies, and so forth.

All this, however, is simply the mythical development of the motif. Its actual career starts within the earthly sphere. It starts with figures, half or even wholly legendary, but linked with, or stemming from, historical events. It starts, in fact, with the fission within magic brought about by Christianity.

Before the rise of Christianity, magic as a whole, that is to say contact with supranatural powers—conjuring, soothsaying, healing, miracle-working practices—was a legitimate part, in fact the most important part, of all religious life. From it evolved prophecy as well as medicine. Its validity was first questioned by the Jewish prophets, those who were the true prophets as opposed to the false, the commercial prophets. But as the Gospels tell us even Jesus resorted to miracles, although even here in the story of his temptation and his refusal to work the miracles which the Devil requested of him, we notice a distinction between legitimate and illegitimate traffic with supranatural powers. And the notion of a compact with the Devil seems to have arisen simultaneously: "Again the Devil taketh him up into an exceeding high mountain, and sheweth him all the kingdoms of the world and the glory of them; And saith unto him, All these things will I give thee, if thou wilt fall down and worship me. Then saith Jesus unto him, Get thee hence, Satan: for it is written, Thou shalt worship the Lord thy God, and him only shalt thou serve."[2]

[2] Matthew 4:8-10; cf. also Luke 4:6-7.

This division within magic reflects a dualism which originated even before Christianity, in Persian cosmology and the Zoroastrian concept of a cosmic struggle between the prince of light, Ahura Mazda, and the prince of darkness, Ahura Mainyush. The struggle is also waged between their respective attendants, the Angels and the Devils. Both kinds of spirits, the Angels (from Greek: *angelos* = messenger) and the Devils (from Greek: *diabolos* = opponent), or at least the idea of two such sharply polarized forces, originated in Persia. Few world-views were of greater and more lasting consequence than the Zoroastrian, with its Mithraistic and Manichaean offshoots. These influenced the ideas and beliefs of the whole Christian underground, from Gnosticism to the Albigensian and Waldensian heresies and to European mysticism. However, the Persian Magi, a Median priestly caste whose name lives on in the word *magic*, were not responsible for that division of magical activities into beneficent and evil contacts with the supranatural, into white magic and black magic. The division arose in the first centuries of the Christian era, in the violent battle of Christian orthodoxy against its enemies. These enemies were, at first, the pagan deities, which were degraded to devils, as becomes evident in I Corinthians 10:20: "But I say that the things which the Gentiles sacrifice, they sacrifice to devils, and not to God, and I would not that ye should have fellowship with devils." We see the traces of this process in certain well-known attributes of the Devil: the goat's hoof, and the horns of Pan and the satyrs, the limping of Hephaistos, the trident of Poseidon, etc.

It is against this background that we have to view the

actual ancestor of the figure, and indeed the name, of Doctor Faustus. This man, Simon Magus, the first conspicuous example of the black magician, whose historicity is probable but not quite certain, lived—if he ever lived—in the time of the apostles[3] and was held to be the founder of Gnosticism, a semi-religious, semi-philosophical movement which was for centuries the most influential and dangerous contestant of early Christianity. Gnosticism was an arch-heresy, the first to challenge the Church; its system of ideas contained, along with Jewish and Christian concepts, all sorts of Persian, Babylonian, Egyptian, and Greek ingredients. It was a characteristically Hellenistic product, a syncretistic mixture of the most diverse elements of speculation, mystery, mythology, and religious dogma.

The Gnostics held that matter is inherently evil—a belief, incidentally, that was shared by Paul. This belief, stemming from Persian dualism, reflected on the position of God the Father, the creator of the material world, who was lowered in his status within the celestial hierarchy. It also led to an increased dissatisfaction with humanity, and the desire to improve upon it by artificial, magical means. This was the starting point for the ceaseless efforts of medieval magicians and nature-philosophers to produce living organisms without resorting to procreation—that is, homunculi. Similarly, the experiments of alchemists (like Fludd, the opponent of Kepler) were not aimed simply at producing gold as the epitome of wealth, but at the liberation of the soul in matter.

Along with his repudiation of matter, Simon Magus

[3] Cf. Acts 8:9-13, 18-24.

went to the extreme of disputing the doctrine of the resurrection of the flesh. According to his system, there was to be only a resurrection of the spirit. It was assumed that man's spiritual nature was derived from a divine being, who had fallen out of the world of light into the world of darkness. The process of deliverance of this spiritual nature and of the human soul from its imprisonment in matter could be effected only through the intervention of another divine being, a redeemer, who would voluntarily descend among men. Simon questioned the divinity of Jesus. He himself claimed to be this redeemer, the manifestation of the "Standing One," which was the supreme, central principle of Gnostic doctrine. He also claimed to have created a soul that had never inhabited a human body.[4]

His most immediate connection with the Faustus story is this: Simon was associated with a woman who, according to the contemporary—of course unfriendly—sources, was a prostitute from Tyre, and whom he called Helena, not just by hazard, but with a special significance. Gnostic symbolism was predominantly sidereal. He, Simon, the Logos and Redeemer, identified himself with the Sun. Woman, the fallen deity, spirit, and soul of the world, had to be the Moon, *Luna* or (in Greek) *Selene,* Helena. Helena was the human soul, fallen into matter and suffering the last indignities, to the point of "standing for hire in a brothel"; Simon was Mind, bringing about her redemption. In addition, a mythological con-

---

[4] Clementine Recognitions. Book II, Ch. 15, quoted by P. M. Palmer and R. P. More, *The Sources of the Faust Tradition* (New York, 1936), p. 18.

Simon Magus, giving a performance of flying in Rome
before the Emperor Nero in the presence of the Apostles Peter and Paul
Painting by Domingo Valls, Catalan painter from Tortosa, 1366-1400

fusion took place; the novelistic accounts of Simon's life and career, called *Recognitiones*, recognitions (probably dating from the fourth century A.D.), confounded and identified this Helena with Helen of Troy.[5]

Finally, Simon, by means of magic, took on the identity of the father of two of his disciples, Faustinianus (or Faustus), and later adopted the name of Faustus.

Simon was said to have engaged in disputations and magical competition with the apostles Peter and Paul in Rome before the Emperor Nero. Suetonius tells us that he performed a feat of flying for the emperor. The story has it that in the course of this performance he perished in the manner of Icarus. A biography of St. Peter included in the *Legenda Aurea*, a collection of saints' legends compiled in the thirteenth century, gives a description of this event. In the course of Simon's magical contest with St. Peter, "he went up to a high tower, which was on the Capitol, in the face of the emperor and a big crowd, and there, being crowned with laurels, threw himself out from place to place and began to fly in the air. . . . Then said Nero: 'This man is very God and ye [Peter and Paul] be two traitors. . . .' Then said Peter . . . 'I charge and conjure you, ye angels of Sathanas, which bear him in the air, by the name of our Lord Jesus Christ, . . . that ye bear nor sustain him no more but let him fall to the earth.' And anon they let him fall to the ground and brake his neck and head, and he died there forthwith."[6]

Here, in the story of Simon, we have the original pat-

[5] Palmer and More, *op.cit.*, p. 15.
[6] *Legenda Aurea* (by Jacopo de Voragine, Archbishop of Genoa), Life of St. Peter the Apostle, trans. by William Caxton in 1483 (London, 1900).

tern of the Faustus motif. In the legends of St. Cyprian of Antioch (which originated in the fourth century) and of Theophilus of Adana (written probably between A.D. 600 and 850), both of whom dabbled in illicit magic, there is added the feature of the pact with Satan. The legend relates that Theophilus, a steward of the Church, took revenge upon his superiors, who had snubbed him, by means of a compact with the Devil written with his own blood. Theophilus is an interesting case, since here was a sinner restored to the Grace of God through the intercession of the Holy Virgin. This represents one of the earliest tributes to the Virgin Mary "Eternal womanhood leads us on high" ("Das Ewig Weibliche zieht uns hinan") as the last lines of Goethe's *Faust* express it.

History offers an endless parade of figures, legendary or actual, who carried the motif farther; among them were no less than eighteen black popes, as well as Robert, Duke of Normandy (Robert the Devil, ca. A.D. 1000), who was reported to have been consecrated to Satan by his mother even before his birth. There was also Gilles de Raiz, companion-in-arms of Joan of Arc, ogre and blue-beard, who by his own confession concluded such a pact with the Devil and was eventually hanged and his body burned as was the custom with repentant sinners. All through the Middle Ages, men lived in a twilight between the divine and the demonic: off and on, the millennium was expected to materialize and this according to old prophecies was to be preceded by the appearance of the Antichrist, bearing the features and imitating the deeds of Christ himself. So people saw in various figures —popes and princes—most conspicuously in the Hohenstaufen emperor Frederick II, the initiator of the millennium, and were never quite sure whether it was the Antichrist or Christ himself who had appeared.

We may now consider the crucial figure, Johannes or Georg Sabellicus Helmstedter, who, inspired by a new edition of the Simonian "Recognitions," represented himself as Faust junior or Faust II. The time was the beginning of the sixteenth century, the period when the Church broke asunder, when humanism, secular thinking, science, and natural philosophy were flourishing. In all this spiritual and intellectual turmoil, the borderlines between science and the magic arts were still fluid. Great thinkers like Kepler, Tycho de Brahe, and Paracelsus concerned themselves with semi-magical procedures; mysticism and demonology were rampant, witches' trials were the order of the day, and the popular imagination battened on the theme of magic and supranatural powers. All of this at least partly accounts for the tremendous and disproportionate popularity of that quack and braggart, the original Doctor Faustus. His magical skills seem to have been rather paltry, but thanks to his remarkable self-advertising, he achieved fame. He hailed himself as "the fount of necromancy" and chief of astrologers, as the most learned alchemist of all times, as the second magus, expert palmist, water-diviner and crystal-gazer, as an infallible prophet and the philosopher of philosophers. He asserted that Christ's miracles were mere trifles compared to his, and that he would be able to reproduce all the works of Plato and Aristotle should they ever be forgotten, and, what is more, improve on them.

He himself boasted of his pact with the Devil; and although he was spurned and denounced by any learned persons who happened to come into contact with him, this did not in any way detract from his reputation. For the fact that he, just like Faustus senior—Simon Magus —was simultaneously a diabolist and a charlatan did not imply a contradiction: The "Father of Lies" was supposed to work through trickery and deceit.

The legacy of his popularity was the pseudobiographical compilation of anecdotes and stories dealing with this Doctor Faustus which was published by Spies in 1587. This book, which drew upon the motifs of all earlier Faustus stories eked out with details from current magical practices and experiences, has become the basis of all subsequent Faustus literature. Even Thomas Mann follows it closely in describing certain crucial stages of Adrian Leverkühn's career.

Let us examine the most striking features of Faust's life and adventures, as related in the Spies book, which have become the classic elements of any Faustus story since.

There is, first, one peculiarity, which is particularly interesting with regard to the portrait of Adrian Leverkühn. The Spies book relates that Faust was of humble but respectable parentage, but so precociously clever that a wealthy relative adopted him and paid for his schooling and university studies. Here, then, is the psychological genesis of an aspiring, arrogant, and perverted mind turning from theology to black magic.

The second important feature is, of course, the pact with the Devil. So swiftly, says the Spies book, did Faust advance in the art of magic that he was soon in a position to trace the magic circle and to summon up an evil spirit. Only a few nights later he signed a pact with him, sealed with his own blood, renouncing Christianity and selling his soul in return for power and knowledge. It should be noted that knowledge, apart from the motive of sheer curiosity, here means foreknowledge, the gift of prophecy, this too as an instrument of power.

There is, thirdly, the recurrent feature of extensive travels, not only all over the globe but transcendent travels upward and downward, into the heights and the depths, with visits to Paradise and Hell, to pope and emperor, to practically all imaginable spheres. These extravagant undertakings include classical necromancy, the summoning up of Greek heroes and figures from the epics —a manifestation of the humanistic enthusiasm for Greek poetry. As far back as the fifteenth century, Joannes Franciscus, a nephew of Pico della Mirandola, reported the conjuring up of Achilles and Hector by a sorcerer, who also recreated the siege of Troy and was thereafter carried off by the Devil. And here, too, comes the revival of the Helena motif: Mephostophiles (such is the first spelling of the name, its origin is unknown) furnishes Faustus with a whole harem of mortal women among whom is the spirit whom he believed to be Helen of Troy. For Helen of Troy had become part and parcel of popular folklore. According to the *Historia* of Hans Sachs, the Nürnberg shoe- and verse-maker, a sorcerer produced Helen of Troy for the entertainment of the Emperor Maximilian I, a motif later used by Goethe.

I leave aside such little items as the Devil's taking the shape of a dog or a pig, and so forth. Only one last element from the popular Faust Book, which found its way into Christopher Marlowe's and into Thomas Mann's Dr. Faustus, requires stressing. It is the last supper—an inversion of Christ's Last Supper—to which Faust invites his dearest friends the night before he is due to be summoned by the Devil. He tells them of his wicked life, of his pact with the Devil, and of his approaching end. And he warns them in the most moving terms to avoid a similar fate: "I die both as a bad and a good Christian. A good Christian because I feel true repentance and cease not to pray for mercy in my heart, so that my soul might yet be saved. A bad Christian, for I know that the Devil will have my body and that I will willingly give it to him if he but leave my soul in peace. Wherefore I beseech you to retire to your beds, and I wish you a good night; but for myself a vexed, bad and terrible one."[7] So it came to pass, and he was duly visited with elaborate horrors and frightful mutilation.

Numerous versions of the theme appeared in the following centuries, all directly or indirectly indebted to the Faust Book of 1587. The Faustus story continued to stir the Christian imagination and conscience up to our day in popular representations and puppet shows (in which form it came the way of Goethe in his youth) which mingled the grotesque, even burlesque, with the gruesome. The Devil, whose power was supposed to be restricted to the earthly sphere, is—like the Persian Ahura Manu (*ahriman*)—unable to foresee all of the effects of his acts or to grasp the spiritual scope of man's

[7] J. Scheible, *Das Kloster*, Stuttgart 1845-49, Vol. II, p. 1066, quoted by E. M. Butler, *The Myth of the Magus* (Cambridge, 1948), p. 137.

thoughts and existence. He is, therefore, liable to be foiled in the end. Then again, as the spirit of negation and derision, he excels in irony. Thus, from as early as the fifteenth century when secular plays began to branch off from the clerical and miracle plays, the Devil assumed the character of a merrymaking rogue, a cheated cheat, or "biter bit," and forebear of the popular stage figure of the jester and buffoon, the harlequin, or *Hanswurst.*

In the meantime, secularization grew and conflicts developed between deeply rooted Christian piety and the new strain of rational enlightenment. The Faustus motif proved especially relevant to this inner struggle. As a result, the story began to be raised to higher levels and to disclose its vast symbolic potentialities.

Christopher Marlowe's play represents the first stage of this process. It is based on a somewhat free English version of the German Faustbook of 1587: *The History of the Damnable life and deserved Death of Doctor John Faustus.* The play follows the popular story fairly closely, even to the coarse and brutal pranks and mischief performed by the diabolist and his devils. However there are certain passages, especially in the grandiose and pathetic scenes at the end, where we feel the traditional denouement overlaid by a very personal shudder, an anxiety springing from a deeper spiritual source, from a longing for faith, perhaps, and from a new loneliness, forsakenness, which this atheistic libertine, Marlowe, may have felt within a still thoroughly Christian world. This shudder is entirely lacking in Goethe's tragedy, but it reappears, in very different circumstances, in Thomas Mann's novel.

Marlowe's play, nevertheless, is still merely an individual story, the more thrilling and gruesome for taking place on the border of salvation. His Faustus is still intent on power in its crudest sense, for the tangible yields of power:

> O what a world of profit and delight,
> Of power, of honour, and omnipotence,
> Is promised to the studious artisan!

And the evil spirit wins him over to his side with prospects like this:

> Be thou on earth as Jove is in the sky,
> Lord and commander of these elements.

Even knowledge is no more than an instrument of power:

> Emperors and Kings,
> Are but obeyed in their several provinces,
> Nor can they raise the wind, nor rend the clouds;
> But his dominion that exceeds in this,
> Stretcheth as far as doth the mind of man;
> A sound magician is a demi-god;
> Here, tire my brains to get a deity!

The impetus of a genius raised the story from the earthly level of Marlowe's play to the entirely spiritual plane of Goethe's tragedy. Here, the vast implications of the motif are unfolded: Doctor Faustus becomes the symbol of modern man.

But before turning to Goethe's work, we must dwell for a moment on the interesting Faustus fragment of

Gotthold Ephraim Lessing, the German champion of enlightenment. His version represents a bridge between the rather pedestrian treatments of the motif in the previous centuries to its later sublimation. Unfortunately, all that is left of Lessing's Faust play, or plays, is one scene, a synopsis, and some secondhand reports. But in these sketchy remnants of his project, one feature stands out that is of particular importance in regard to the further developments of the theme, and especially in regard to Thomas Mann's version. This is the new high value set upon knowledge and wisdom, which reflects the ascendancy of rationalism. Up to the Renaissance, extra-theological knowledge had been considered in itself a rather dangerous and sinful commodity. Indeed, the compact with the Devil was seen as the effect rather than the cause of a person's concern with secular knowledge, the truth being found exclusively in the teachings of the divine. In Lessing's plot, Satan calls together his sub-devils to hear what they have found in the way of some juicy morsel among the humans who would make a prospective victim. Topping all these reports is the one on Faustus, God's darling, a pure, lonely youth, wholly devoted to wisdom, renouncing all passion except the one for truth, and in the opinion of Satan's scout "extremely dangerous for you and us, if he ever became a teacher of the people. . . ." This is a genuine statement of enlightenment, implying as it does that the Devil can be defeated by truth. But the Devil himself takes issue with this optimism and this, in fact, marks the crucial turn, the intimation of a new experience and the birth of modern Faustianism. Satan asks of his underling: "Doesn't he possess thirst of knowledge?" "More than any mortal," is the reply. "Then, you fool," Satan says, "just leave him to me. This is sufficient to ruin a man." And this accords with a passage in one of the surviving scenes, as quoted in Lessing's seventeenth "Letter on Literature" (*Literaturbrief*), where Faust is to choose among the seven quickest infernal spirits. He picks the one who claims to be as fast as the transition from good to evil: "Yes, indeed," says Faust, "nothing is faster than that—I experienced it myself." This notion contains in the bud the realization of the paradox of the human situation, indeed of life itself, which plays such a prominent role in Goethe's and in all the recent versions of the story.

Goethe's protagonist is no longer any concrete, specific individual, but a mythical figure representing and encompassing man as such, Western man, modern man, dynamic man, restless, impatient, urged forward by a relentless drive of self-enlargement, of self-expansion—a drive that pushes him farther and farther, deeper and higher into the cosmic, the spiritually cosmic sphere. All the new resources of modern thinking and scholarship have been pressed into service—in fact, this great poem is a compendium of the vastly developed intellectual material of Goethe's age. It is Goethe's final attempt to comprehend the whole of his world, to do so explicitly as well as synthetically. Hence it is one of the earliest, perhaps— with *Wilhelm Meisters Wanderjahre—the* earliest great literary work to assume that cryptically abstract character which inevitably marks all important works of art of our day.

However, the stuff of human knowledge, although its

traces appear throughout the play, has been essentially exhausted and left behind by Faust even before the action starts. It is no longer power as such, in its material sense; it is no longer that cosmic imperialism of Marlowe's magician that Goethe's Faust is bent on. It is not knowledge as a means to power, as a means to enjoy the palpable gifts of the world; in fact it is not knowledge at all in the usual, external, and extensive sense of the word. It is an entirely different kind of knowledge. In his urge toward self-aggrandizement Faust does not aim at the world. He seeks himself, a higher and deeper self; he seeks the fullness of life, the fullness of the moment, that tension-filled blend of joy and suffering which life actually is. Here is what Faust tells Mephistopheles:

> *Du hörest ja, von Freud ist nicht die Rede*
> *Dem Taumel weih ich mich, dem schmerzlichsten*
> > *Genuss,*
> *Verliebtem Hass, erquickendem Verdruss.*
> *Mein Busen, der von Wissensdrang geheilt ist,*
> *Soll keinen Schmerzen künftig sich verschliessen*
> *Und was der ganzen Menschheit zugeteilt ist*
> *Will ich in meinem inneren Selbst geniessen,*
> *Mit meinem Geist das Höchst und Tiefste greifen,*
> *Ihr Wohl and Weh auf meinen Busen häufen,*
> *Und so mein eigen Selbst zu ihrem Selbst erweitern*
> *Und, wie sie selbst, am End auch ich zerscheitern.*

I've told you, it is no question of happiness.
The most painful joy, enamored hate, enlivening
Disgust—I devote myself to all excess.
My breast, now cured of its appetite for knowledge,

From now is open to all and every smart,
And what is allotted to the whole of mankind
That will I sample in my inmost heart,
Grasping the highest and lowest with my spirit,
Piling men's weal and woe upon my neck,
To extend myself to embrace all human selves
And to founder in the end, like them, a wreck.[8]

This is what he asks from his Devil. From these crucial lines we gather that he cares neither for simple joy
—"enjoyment makes debased," he replies to Mephistopheles' offers—nor does he give a fig for what may happen
after life, be it Heaven or Hell.

> *Das Drüben kann mich wenig kümmern ...*
> *Aus dieser Erde quillen meine Freuden,*
> *Und diese Sonne scheinet meinen Leiden;*
> *Kann ich mich erst von ihnen scheiden,*
> *Dann mag, was will und kann, geschehn:*
> *Davon will ich nichts weiter hören ...*

> Of the beyond I have no thought ...
> My joys come from this earth, and there,
> That sun has burnt on my despair:
> Once I have left those, I don't care:
> What happens is of no concern[9]

So he does not reach out for anything beyond this life
on earth. But he has high requirements for this earthly
life. He wants to embrace the beyond, the transcendental,
the divine even in the Here and Now. This is what he
understands by the fullness of the moment. Its fullness,
its transcendence is inherent in its transience.

[8] Translated by Louis MacNeice.
[9] Translated by Walter Kaufmann.

> *Werd ich zum Augenblicke sagen:*
> *Verweile doch, du bist so schön!*
> *Dann magst du mich in Fesseln schlagen,*
> *Dann will ich gern zugrundegehn.*

> If ever I say to the passing moment
> "Linger a while! Thou art so fair!"
> Then you may cast me into fetters,
> I will gladly perish then and there![10]

and again:

> *Im Weiterschreiten find er Qual und Glück*
> *Er! Unbefriedigt jeden Augenblick.*

> In marching onwards, bliss and torment find
> Though, every moment, with unsated mind![11]

Only in his last moment, his very moment of passing, he has a pre-vision of a moment that is not passing: the moment surpassingly surviving in the lasting "traces of his earthly days:"

> *Im Vorgefühl von solchem hohen Glück*
> *Geniess ich jetzt den höchsten Augenblick.*

> As I now presage a happiness so high
> I now enjoy the highest moment...[12]

So to Faust the moment is both transient and transcendent. This transcendence of the moment was what he wanted to hold and behold throughout his life—a consummate paradox, the paradox of paradoxes. And the core of this tragedy, that which makes it a tragedy, is

---

[10] Translated by Louis MacNeice.
[11] Translated by Bayard Taylor.
[12] Translated by Walter Kaufmann.

man's powerlessness to attain this condition. A forefeeling of it in the moment of his passing—this is all, at best, that he can achieve, and thus life's highest moment appears to be death.

Man's life is a paradox, and its paradoxicality cannot be resolved except through the working of Grace. Yet, in Goethe's tragedy—and this turns it, in the old, Dantesque sense into a comedy—the intervention of Grace is certain, it is even predestined, thanks to a single factor. This factor is the stake in God's wager with Mephistopheles. It is expressed by the Lord at the beginning of the play:

> *Ein guter Mensch in seinem dunkeln Drange*
> *Ist sich des rechten Weges wohl bewusst*

> A good man with his groping intuitions
> Still knows the path that is true and fit[13]

The same faith is proclaimed by the angels at the end:

> *Wer immer strebend sich bemüht*
> *Den können wir erlösen*
> *Und hat an ihm die Liebe gar*
> *Von oben teilgenommen*
> *Begegnet ihm die selige Schar*
> *Mit herzlichem Willkommen.*

> Whoever aspires unweariedly
> Is not beyond redeeming
> And if he feels the grace of love
> That from On High is given
> The Blessed Hosts that wait above
> Shall welcome him to Heaven![14]

[13] Translated by Louis MacNeice.
[14] Translated by Bayard Taylor.

As in the story of Job, which is the prototype of this framework, the wager hinges on the question of whether Mephistopheles will be able to divert Faust from this aspiration.

Now Faust is not even a good man, by no means. He does the most reprehensible things all through his career and to his very end. But, and this is crucial: although transgressing the limits of humanity, he is not an inhuman man. For all his tricks and seductions Mephistopheles does not manage to extinguish this human feeling in Faust—the sense, the clear distinction, the potential choice, of good and evil. Come what may, aspiration keeps surging up in him, the aspiration toward higher and higher goals, toward the highest goal. This, the essential disposition and destiny of Western man, who may be described as Christian man, as still ultimately with Goethe, or as Nordic man, as with Spengler—this unceasing striving and self-expansion beyond the confines of the Here and Now, and yet within the Here and Now —this, characteristically, is the quality most highly prized even by the Lord of the Christian Heaven.

For this grandiose, symbolical, and, in places, even allegorical drama, with all its excursions into the pagan, is still enacted within the framework of a traditionally Christian universe. It is resolved, brought to a happy, a blessed, end by Christian faith. The human paradox still serves as a *quia absurdum* for the act of Grace, for the act of Salvation. Helena, the aphrodisian epitome and revelation of beauty, the incarnation of art and poetry, "the grand significance of fleeting days," dissolves like a mirage. Eros in the grand style gives way to the love of that plain Nordic maiden, Margaret, who becomes one with the Virgin Mary and "leadeth him upward and on." Again aspiration, the ever-striving spirit is the saving faculty.

This was still the time of humanistic, classicistic *Bildung*, of the emergence of the sciences, from romantic spirituality with its universalistic outlook. The border-line between the arts and the sciences was still fluid. It was the time of Hegel and Schelling, when spirit, rational and poetic, was held in highest esteem. Goethe was the last to hold this intellectual universe together. The cultural climate of our present world, one hundred and fifty years later, is very different. The Christian Heaven is deserted; it is replaced by astrophysical infinities, by the skies, the stratosphere, ionosphere, exosphere, into which we launch our satellites and rockets. There is no haven, no resting place, no boundary in sight. The humanistic universe has broken asunder, the sciences have immensely expanded and grown apart from each other. They have become specialized and functionalized; they have parted ways with the arts—and where is philosophy? Its remains are existentialism and the various kinds of logic (symbolic, linguistic, analytical). While rationalism triumphs in the many corners of science and technology, human reason as a controlling force is fading away. Intellect, thinking, spirit, have been utterly discredited not only by the catastrophes and crises but also by the comforts of our century. Between the artist, the man of Mind and his society, a terrible rift has developed. This had already begun to happen in Goethe's time—Goethe himself felt it and suffered under it. The estrangement was accentuated by the artists and thinkers themselves who found themselves forced into ever-increasing complexities and abstractions in their effort to cope with the modern world. As a result, art and mind have become problematic to themselves; the problems of form, the questions or perception and expression, have become the substance of art's explorations.

This, then, is the climate into which Thomas Mann was born with his own, very personal problem, which, somatically as it were, contained in itself the cultural problem of his age. The note is first sounded in his early story, *Tonio Kröger* which treats of the innate conflict between the bourgeois and the artist, the inevitable, inborn alienation of the artist from the common world and its blond normality. This personal problem of his, together with the corresponding outer problem of the cultural situation in which he grew up, directed Thomas Mann toward the Faustus motif. To him, Faustus represents the most highly developed exponent of his arch-experience; he appears as a cosmic Tonio Kröger, a Tonio Kröger raised to an ultimate epochal and human significance.

The central theme is this: The modern artist in his endeavor to render the staggering complex experience of modern life, in his striving for truth and the genuine form of expression that truth demands, in his flight from the banal and commonplace, the already said and done, is carried into spheres of abstraction far remote from the community of men. Aiming at absolute truth, he attempts to grasp the whole, to recreate, or rather, to *create* a whole out of the chaos of a disjointed world. His reward for this is to be expelled from the paradise of love, from ordinary communion with ordinary men, the "Thou with Mankind." Thus, the purest form of being, Mind, has become sin. The new fall of man is a rise, the ascent into the extreme of abstraction. The Icarian ruin of Adrian Leverkühn, the new Faustus, comes about through the disease contracted from uniting with a whore. Love, the purest love, flares up at the most casual physical contact, and love, which from the first was forbidden the genius, contains the poison, the demoniac involvement, the consummation of the Mephistophelian pact.

To be sure, even in Goethe's Faust there is a full recognition of the paradox of earthly life: the ever-striving, self-expanding, self-transcending spirit is by that very token unable to fulfill its destiny. But for Goethe the norm still stands, the long established values stand whose relation to each other and to the human being are clearly defined. A norm exists, not down below, conventionalized in a world of middle-class normality, but high above, in the sphere of a Christian Heaven. The Faustian destiny is seen from above, from the height of this Christian norm, and it is oriented upward. This is the meaning of the whole celestial framework, the "Prologue in Heaven" and the reception into Heaven. Human aspiration, the human spirit, although infinite in its earthly course, has a final haven, a supremely objective measure, in which it is transcendentally contained, and indeed gives it its authorization.

For Adrian Leverkühn no such above and beyond, no such measure and haven and authorization, is any longer available. His tragedy is seen from below, and in relation to a below. His problem is the relation of mind to its common basis, to the human community from which it is divorced. Sin is no longer the breach of an absolute norm, rather it is the Adamitic break with the community of creatures. Adrian Leverkühn is cut off from the community of his fellow-men. What there is of Heaven is just as internalized as what there is of Hell—on the one hand there is the ecstasy of artistic creation, on the other hand the disease as punishment of a biologized sin. Mind, in its isolation and desolation, builds its own Heaven, and has to pay for it with its own Hell. Indeed, in the career of a mind relegated to its own infinity, there is hardly any clear distinction between Heaven and Hell, between Good and Evil, for both are tainted by each other—the good being a *Fleur du Mal* and vice versa. Discipline itself, that old instrument of the norm, has become in *Doctor Faustus* a thing of the devil, an affair of magic. The paradox is complete and remains unresolved. Here Grace, which had brought deliverance to Goethe's Faust, is merely a dim "hope beyond hopelessness," a "transcendence of despair."

This paradox, this immanence of Heaven and Hell in man, this inextricable mingling of Good and Evil in all existence, this is the new experience that dominates the recent treatments of the Faustus motif.

In Paul Valéry's existentialist farce, *Mon Faust*, the Devil is altogether antiquated, an anachronism. He is no match for the human being, for human existence in its self-contained hell. And he freezes himself out of existence in the icy mountain air of the absolutely single, lonely man, the *solitaire* who can no longer stand the infectious company of other human beings. For Faust, "there is neither hot, nor cold . . . there is no high, nor low. . . . And there is an enormous amount of nothing in the All."

Jean-Paul Sartre's play *Le diable et le bon dieu* ("The Devil and the good Lord") is set in an imaginary sixteenth century, the period of the German peasants' wars and of the original Doctor Faustus. Its action takes place in the socio-political sphere and bears a distinct reference to the problems of our day and more specifically to the personal dilemma of Sartre himself, leaning toward communism, but repelled by the party dogma and the party line, longing for contact with the workers, but rejected by them as an intellectual. The play is, as he himself indicated, a sequel and metaphysical extension of his former play *Les mains sales* ("Dirty Hands") and like that play, which dealt with the problem more directly and explicitly, it implies a renunciation of ideology, and with it, renunciation of the absolute.

Sartre's Faustus, whom he calls Goetz, in an allusion to the German knight Goetz von Berlichingen who led the peasants in their revolt, is torn between his dual nature of nobleman and peasant and is rejected by both parties. At first Goetz behaves like a cynical Renaissance despot, intent on doing evil as an absolute, not for any gain, not even for the sake of power, but simply for destruction per se. But what he destroys are merely human individuals, not the social order or the social classes, and in the end his evil-doing benefits the ruling powers. When he then proposes to do the absolute good, this again turns out to be futile. He gives his lands away to the peasants who do not understand his act because his language and terms are not theirs, and his benefactions give rise to a general war in which everything is lost. So in seeking the absolute in both the evil and the good, he has accomplished nothing but the destruction of human lives.

The theme of this tragedy is the breakdown of the absolute. Pitted against Goetz is an incarnation of the old Faustus, who significantly is called Heinrich. He is a priest who while intellectually experimenting with doubt struggles to preserve the reality of the suprahuman absolute, in both its forms of God and the Devil. He wants a higher judge of his actions than men. Between him and Goetz, between the old and the new Faustus, the crucial dialogues take place.

What Sartre arrives at is essentially the dissolution of the absolute. "God," says Goetz, "is the void over our heads, God is silence, God is absence, God is the loneliness of man." And even for Heinrich "the Devil is never there when one needs him." "There was no one but myself," says Goetz, "it is I who have cheated, who have worked miracles; it is myself whom I accuse today, and I am the only one who is able to absolve man. I, man. Good-bye monsters, good-bye saints! . . . There is no one but men, human beings." As for these human beings, Goetz has discovered that "I must accept my part of their crimes if I want to have my part of their love and of their virtues. . . . On this earth and in this time, the Good and the Bad are inseparable: I consent to be bad in order to become good."

These somber experiences and insights of some of the most penetrating minds of our age are only too understandable when we contemplate our present world. The absolute has vanished. No longer do we strive after the absolute, after any ultimate goal; goals have revealed their futility. What we pursue is the limitless. The limitless has become the secular absolute, our absolute. We are reaching for the moon, no longer metaphorically but in practical reality. Yet in the frenzied pursuit of an arrogant technology, we are losing our human ground. It is being abandoned to intellectual, moral, and political anarchy. Indeed, in our day Doctor Faustus has become, in a terrifying way, the symbol of modern man. For unless we achieve a human community, all the rest of our glorious achievements will turn out to have been a pact with the Devil.

1957

INDEX